SMALL
SPIRITS

NATIVE AMERICAN DOLLS
FROM THE NATIONAL MUSEUM
OF THE AMERICAN INDIAN

BY MARY JANE LENZ

SMITHSONIAN

NATIONAL MUSEUM OF THE AMERICAN INDIAN

WASHINGTON, D.C., AND NEW YORK

IN ASSOCIATION WITH

UNIVERSITY OF WASHINGTON PRESS

SEATTLE AND LONDON

Small Spirits: Native American Dolls from the National Museum of the American Indian is a revised, augmented, and updated edition, including all new photography, of *The Stuff of Dreams: Native American Dolls*, originally published in 1986.

Head of Publications: Terence Winch
Editor: Elizabeth Kennedy Gische
Designer: Steve Bell
Design Assistant: Renu Pavate

The Smithsonian's National Museum of the American Indian is dedicated to working in collaboration with the indigenous peoples of the Americas to protect and foster Native cultures throughout the Western Hemisphere. The museum's publishing program seeks to augment awareness of Native American beliefs and lifeways, and to educate the public about the history and significance of Native cultures.

For information about the Smithsonian's National Museum of the American Indian, visit the NMAI Website at www.AmericanIndian.si.edu.

University of Washington Press
PO Box 50096
Seattle, WA 98145-5096
www.washington.edu/uwpress

Printed in China

LIBRARY OF CONGRESS
CATALOGING-IN-PUBLICATION DATA
Lenz, Mary Jane.
Small spirits : Native American dolls from the Smithsonian National Museum of the American Indian / by Mary Jane Lenz.
Rev. ed. of : The stuff of dreams. ©1986.
Includes bibliographical references.
ISBN 0-295-98363-9
1. National Museum of the American Indian (U.S.)-Exhibitions. 2. Indian dolls-Exhibitions.
E59.D66L46   2004
745.592'21'08997007471-dc22

2003062147

Front Cover (left to right): Doll representing an Aymara Carnaval dancer (detail); see figure 79. Cochiti Pueblo figure depicting a natty cowboy (detail); see figure 91. Yup'ik doll representing a woman making a circular mat of beach grass (detail); see figure 100. Teton Lakota woman doll (detail); see figure 1. Tohono O'odham basketry doll (detail); see figure 93.

Back Cover: Master potter Helen Cordero began the modern tradition of Storyteller dolls in the 1960s and inspired two generations of ceramic artists to experiment with the form. Cordero's Storytellers were inspired by her grandfather who, she remembers, was always surrounded by children listening to his wonderful stories. *25/9180*

Inside Cover: Pretty Beads, a Crow girl, carries her doll and cradleboard fastened to the pommel of her horse's saddle. *N41420*

Title page: This prize-winning tableau by Lakota artist Emil Her Many Horses is titled *Honoring Our Lakota Vietnam Veterans. 26/604*

CONTENTS

THE TOYS AND TOOLS OF LIFE

STATUES, EFFIGIES, SCARECROWS— three-dimensional likenesses of the human form, created for all manner of reasons, have been popular for tens of thousands of years. But perhaps no member of this cast of characters speaks so directly to the human heart as does the doll. And I would argue that the special intimacy and affection reserved for dolls is profoundly connected to their association with childhood.

For indigenous peoples, the meaning and importance of dolls is further enhanced by a belief central to Native life, which holds that objects of cultural significance possess their own spirits. This belief clearly extends very directly to dolls, whose anthropomorphic form immediately suggests such inner life.

In *Small Spirits: Native American Dolls from the National Museum of the American Indian*, you will be treated to an insightful, learned, and entertaining exploration of these wondrous objects, which are among the most enchanting of the grand multitude of works in the museum's vast collection.

A telling story in *The New Yorker* by the extraordinarily gifted writer Louise Erdrich (Turtle Mountain Band of Chippewa) captures, I think, something central in the attitude Indians have toward dolls. The story's narrator, an estate appraiser, comes upon an Indian doll while going through the contents of a house. After giving an exquisitely detailed description of the doll, Erdrich offers this conversation between the narrator and the grandniece of the house's deceased owners:

Figure 1. The pristine quality of this Teton Lakota doll suggests that it may have been made for show rather than play. It reveals a remarkable amount of ethnographic detail. The long double earrings and choker are fashioned from porcupine quills to resemble dentalium shell jewelry worn throughout the Plains. The shells were traded from the Pacific coast. A beaded knife sheath hangs from the belt. The doll also wears a muslin underdress, which was often worn underneath a buckskin dress for comfort. *13/7839*

"Oh, there she is!" She took the doll from its wrapping and handled it with familiar tenderness, smoothing the coarse hair down and caressing the slender horsehair brows embroidered above the glittering eyes. "My uncles used to let me play with her if I was very good."

"*She's* very good, you know. Valuable, I mean. We should have a museum curator look at her."

"Yeah?" Sarah was surprised, but not particularly pleased. I think she felt the same way I did about the doll. It was personal—the delight of owning the doll had nothing to do with its worth.

Figure 2. This little Navajo girl was photographed in Ramah, New Mexico, around 1940, making a doll from pine needles and a sugar sack. Photo by Paul J. Woolf. *P24163*

The doll's value is spiritual, not monetary: this core belief is crucial to understanding how we Indians regard the many things of great beauty our ancestors have created. Erdrich's narrator notwithstanding, for this book we have indeed turned to a museum curator to help us plumb the cultural meaning of these objects. That curator is our own Mary Jane Lenz, who has worked with our collection from its days as part of the old Museum of the American Indian in New York to its transformation as one of the cornerstones of the Smithsonian. *Small Spirits* is the revised and rewritten version of Mary Jane's 1986 seminal study of our doll collection, originally called *The Stuff of Dreams*. She brings her customary lucidity to the discussion of these wonderful small spirits, displaying an unrivalled degree of knowledge and authority. With all new photography and design, *Small Spirits* reinvents its 1986 predecessor.

In this book, you will read about the role and significance of hundreds of dolls representing cultures from the Arctic to the Brazilian rain forest. We hope you will come to appreciate the fineness of art and craftsmanship that characterize many of these works. Most of all, we hope you will come away with a greater regard for the ways in which Native peoples have always placed children at the center of their lives. While dolls are often toys or playthings, they have also been serious teaching tools, a way for children to learn essential details and truths about traditional life and culture.

We are very pleased to have *Small Spirits* arrive in time for the opening of our splendid new building on the National Mall, where the dolls pictured in this book will be happily at home and on view in the *Window on Collections: Many Hands, Many Voices* area. I particularly want to thank Mary Jane Lenz for her excellent text, and our former colleague Clara Sue Kidwell (Choctaw/Chippewa) for her superb new introduction.

—W. RICHARD WEST, JR.
(*Southern Cheyenne and member of the Cheyenne and Arapaho Tribes of Oklahoma*)
DIRECTOR, NATIONAL MUSEUM OF THE AMERICAN INDIAN

PREFACE & ACKNOWLEDGMENTS

SMALL SPIRITS IS A NEW, REVISED, and updated version of *The Stuff of Dreams: Native American Dolls*, published in 1986 by the Museum of the American Indian, the forerunner institution to the Smithsonian's National Museum of the American Indian. That earlier edition was the catalogue for a traveling exhibition of the same name funded by the National Endowment for the Humanities. *The Stuff of Dreams* catalogue has long been out of print, but interest in it remained high through the years, and Terence Winch, Head of Publications for the National Museum of the American Indian, conceived the idea of a new edition.

The new edition retains much of the intent of the original—to highlight the hemispheric collection of the museum as well as to explore several ways of looking at and thinking about dolls. *Small Spirits* shows many of the same wonderful dolls that appeared in *The Stuff of Dreams*. But it also includes new ones, particularly some splendid examples from the Indian Arts and Crafts Board Collection that in 1999 was transferred from the Department of the Interior to the National Museum of the American Indian. The Indian Arts and Crafts Board Collection, created as an artistic and economic opportunity for Native people to support themselves during the Great Depression of the 1930s, fostered the careers of a number of potters, carvers, basket-weavers and—as this publication will show—doll makers.

An increased awareness of and sensitivity to the cultural values of Native people is one of the ways the world has changed for the better in the past twenty years. As one indication of that change, certain of the dolls pictured earlier, particularly some used in sacred ceremonies, are omitted from *Small Spirits,* being deemed inappropriate for photography or for presentation to a non-tribal audience. The National Museum of the American Indian is not alone among museums in this changed sensibility, but it has taken a lead by incorporating into its mission and philosophy the centrality of Native voices and wishes in all museum programs and initiatives. As Native people have begun to shape their representation and tell their own stories in museums and cultural centers, they have also shaped the way we look at and think about collections such as the one presented here.

Small Spirits highlights a wide range of dolls from the National Museum of the American Indian collections, ranging from archaeological figurines to contemporary souvenirs made for the tourist trade and sophisticated creations intended for the collectors' market. They represent Native cultures from throughout the Western Hemisphere, from the Arctic to South America. The list of dolls at the back of the book is designed to provide useful information about each doll without interrupting the continuity of the text. The bibliography is targeted for the non-specialist but each reference includes its own substantial bibliography to aid the reader who wishes to delve deeper into a particular topic.

My grateful thanks go out, for their advice and assistance, to many people. In addition to the many individuals mentioned in the first edition, some of whom are now deceased, I want to thank designer Steve Bell for re-imagining the book's visual identity and editor Elizabeth Kennedy Gische for her expert attention to the text. Both of them worked under the able direction of Terence Winch. I am also greatly indebted to Head of Photography Cynthia Frankenburg and to photographers Ernest Amoroso, Katherine Fogden, and Roger Whiteside, whose collective talents help to make this book a stunning visual experience. Special thanks are also due to Charles Bessant, Fran Biehl, Linda Greatorex, Emil Her Many Horses, Jessica Johnson, Leigh J. Kuwanwisiwma, Amber Lincoln, Ann McMullen, Gary Roybal, Susan Secakuku, Dark Rain Thom, and Leslie Wheelock. All errors are mine alone.

—Mary Jane Lenz

INTRODUCTION

WHEN I WAS GROWING UP my mother had a Seminole doll that she had bought at a shop near Tahlequah, Oklahoma. It had a wide brimmed hat, and I was intrigued by the intricacy of the patchwork strips on its dress. The small squares of fabric were neatly joined, and since my grandmother was teaching me to sew on her old Singer sewing machine, I had an idea that it was very difficult to deal with such tiny pieces of material.

My mother has continued to collect dolls over the years, and now she has a crowd of them on shelves in the den. I have bought some of them for her—a pair of Inuit dolls; a man and woman with stone faces for a fiftieth wedding anniversary present; a Pueblo Storyteller doll that I also used as the central image on a poster advertising a summer workshop on American Indian cultures; a Cherokee doll with her mortar and pestle; a Navajo doll seated at a traditional loom. Each of these dolls, and the original Seminole doll in the collection, is rich with memories.

This book began with a 1986 traveling exhibition of dolls from New York City's Museum of the American Indian. The exhibition catalogue displayed the dolls beautifully and explored the wide range of roles they played in Native cultures. That landmark catalogue, authored by Mary Jane Lenz, is the basis for this expanded and updated revisiting of the subject of Native American dolls. Lenz, now a curator at the new National Museum of the American Indian (NMAI), created when the Smithsonian Institution assumed control of the collections of the old Museum of the American Indian,

Figure 3. The Seminole people have used sewing machines to make their colorful patchwork clothing since about 1900. This doll maker produces dolls for sale dressed in miniature patchwork outfits. Photograph by Willard R. Culver. ©1948 National Geographic.

has further enhanced the power and significance of her earlier work by adding important new scholarship and a number of beautiful contemporary dolls by known artists.

Dolls continue to be part of the displays at the National Museum of the American Indian. A Seminole doll similar to my mother's was part of one presentation in *Creation's Journey*, one of the opening exhibitions at the George Gustav Heye Center of NMAI in New York City in November of 1994. The display featured a life-size male mannequin holding a child mannequin by the hand. The child's garment was a replica of the man's patchwork "big shirt." The doll stood in a case nearby.

The display emphasized the universal point that dolls are life in miniature—more than simply playthings but ways of teaching. Katsina dolls teach Hopi children to recognize the various spiritual beings who appear in the ceremonial dances between the winter solstice and mid-July. During the rest of the year katsinas live in their homes in the San Francisco Mountains where they plant and tend their crops. Children learn that Masau'u is the fire god, who brings seeds and makes the crops grow, but to encounter the god face-to-face leads to death. The Natackas are giants who appear at the time of the first snowfall and go from house to house, threatening to carry off children who have been bad. Ethnographic studies of Hopi katsina dolls identified as many as 266. The pantheon of katsinas is not static. New ones may appear with changing customs. Take, for example, the katsina doll in tennis shoes.

Dolls model the roles of men and women in Native societies. In conjunction with the opening of the Heye Center, *Smithsonian* magazine featured a lavish pictorial spread highlighting objects from NMAI's collection. One special photograph was of a miniature tipi with a little doll in a cradleboard propped near the entry, a female doll standing beside the tipi, and a male doll on a horse arriving home. The photo evokes the strong sense of family that characterizes Indian communities. The little cradleboard and its occupant emphasize the value placed upon children and the honor women achieved in their roles as mothers. Three Aleut male dolls ride in a miniature *baidarka*, a three-man animal skin kayak, the lead man's paddle poised above the invisible sea. Their eyes are shaded from the glare by wooden hats, carefully painted and decorated. The hats' aesthetic qualities were intended to appeal to the animals that

Figure 4. Toy tipis were still being played with in the 1930s and 1940s, as seen in this photograph of Kiowa children at a mission school in Anadarko, Oklahoma. *P20438*

the men hunted. The baidarka and its passengers modeled the behavior of Aleut men.

Dolls may also symbolize fertility. In his autobiography, *Sun Chief*, Don Talayesva (Hopi) describes how small dolls were buried as offerings with a hawk that was killed to free its spirit so it could return the next year and hatch many young. Storyteller dolls with open mouths and crowds of children in their arms show the relationship between human speech as a powerful and creative act and the bearing of children. Storytelling is not simply for amusement. It teaches, and in cultures that value the act of speaking over the printed page, it is the primary form of instruction.

Dolls can be made of the simplest of materials. Some of my mother's favorite dolls are small angels made of cornhusks folded over and tied to form the head and then split to make wings. These dolls hung on the Christmas tree for several years until, with no

Figure 5. Anna Martins of Chevak, Alaska, created this droll, wrinkled old man dressed in the traditional waterproof hooded raincoat worn by hunters in kayaks. "Making ugly faces" is part of the fun at parties and dances among the people of southwest Alaska, and the doll maker may here be making reference to this practice. *25/5741*

children around to help her, my mother finally gave up decorating a tree. The deep pink hollyhock blooms from my grandmother's garden in our backyard could be turned inside out so the large stamen formed the body, and the petals formed a lovely bell-shaped skirt. There are charming old lady dolls whose wrinkled faces are made of dried apples. In the late nineteenth century, china and bisque headed dolls, obviously of American origin, became fairly common. Dressed in Native clothing styles, ensconced in cradleboards, and wearing Indian ornaments, they were transformed into Indian dolls.

Dolls can also be quite elaborate, with exquisite detailing of dress and ornaments. My mother's Navajo weaver doll wears the typical velvet overblouse and satin skirt. She has a tiny silver concho belt and turquoise necklace. Her loom is suspended from a highly polished branch of cedar and contains a partially finished rug. Many dolls from Plains tribes wear tiny beaded moccasins and heavily beaded buckskin dresses. Bone and shell jewelry is common. On a Blackfoot doll, small white beads on the dark bodice of the doll's dress represent the elk teeth that were a sign of the status and prestige of a woman's family. The story is that only the two eyeteeth of the elk were used for such decorations, and the rows and rows of them displayed on the dress indicated the hunting prowess of the woman's male relatives. Such a doll required much time to make. Women could show off their beading skills and teach their daughters the meaning of prestige in their societies.

The importance of traditional garments is still apparent in Indian princess competitions. The contestants in the Miss Choctaw pageant in Pearl River, Mississippi (one of the reservation communities of the Mississippi Band of Choctaw Indians), wear ruffled floor-length cotton dresses with patchwork strip trim and beaded collars. Part of the competition is each contestant's description of which of her relatives made her dress and beadwork. The judgment is ultimately not on the girl's individual talent and beauty, but on the skills of her extended family.

The elaboration of these dolls makes them in one sense works of art, worthy of display in museums. It also, as with the Blackfeet doll, allows them to represent the ideals of Indian societies. Dignity and pride are exemplified in elegantly made and decorated garments. I recall going to Crow Fair in Montana one summer. This event is one of the major powwows on the summer circuit. It is held near Crow Agency on the Crow Reservation. The Crow people are generally superb equestrians. Horses roamed freely around the powwow grounds, and young children would often race up to a horse and mount bareback with a single bound. The thrill of the Grand Entry was seeing a group of Crow people parade into the grounds on their horses, the men in feather war bonnets and buckskins, the women in elaborately beaded buckskin dresses, and some in dark cloth dresses decorated with rows of elk teeth. The Crow are a proud people, and that pride was tangible in their bearing and their garments.

Dolls may represent ideals, but they also stir the imagination. Some dolls do not have faces, and a Seneca man once explained that this allows children to imagine anything they want about the doll's appearance and character. Rather than having an identity imposed upon it, such a doll can have a life of its own through the creative act of imagining in a child's mind. Contrast one of these unique dolls with a contemporary Barbie doll, elaborately coiffed, with a full wardrobe and an extraordinary array of accessories, including houses, cars, and a boyfriend named Ken. The Barbie doll leaves virtually nothing to the imagination.

Dolls appear in a wide range of situations in Indian cultures. They are used in ceremonies to represent spiritual power. Jointed dolls in Northwest Coast ceremonies represented spiritual beings, and on the Makah reservation on the Olympic Peninsula in the state of Washington, children learn about Quesate, a creator, through puppet shows that feature his exploits. The movable figures imply a sense of power that can imbue dolls made of inanimate materials with personality. The ability of a doll to move also implies its power to transform into a spiritual being or a human being.

This power of transformation is an essential aspect of power in Native societies. If the doll represents humanity, and if imagination can see the doll as having personality, then perhaps the doll can be really alive. As katsina dolls come alive when the katsina dancers appear in Hopi villages, they bridge the gap between the imaginary and the real. Jointed dolls, sometimes in the form of puppets, were used in ceremonies on the Northwest Coast. In the darkness of a long house lit by a blazing bonfire in the center of the floor, the figures could well appear to have a life of their own.

Along with my mother's Seminole doll, I had Raggedy Ann and Andy dolls. They were the result of a very popular series of children's books. As a voracious reader, I absorbed the importance of the candy hearts that were supposedly imbedded in their cloth chests, which would allow the love of a child to bring them to real life. Characters such as Pinocchio, the puppet who wants to be a boy, or the Tin Man in *The Wizard of Oz*, who only wants a heart, show this emphasis on the primacy of human life. The notion of dolls becoming alive, as in the stories of Raggedy Ann and Andy, depended on human love. In Native societies, movable dolls could effect their own spiritual transformation. My mother's Seminole doll and thousands—perhaps hundreds of thousands—like it, were made for the tourist trade. Katsina dolls are sold in multitudes in museum gift shops, primarily in the Southwest but virtually

throughout the country. They have become one of the major exemplars of what most museum visitors probably perceive as a kind of generic Indian culture. Plastic, light-skinned dolls sport pseudo-buckskin garments, feathers in their hair, and beaded headbands to represent Plains Indians. In some cases, the skin is dark, but the dolls are obviously mass-produced, and they represent the stereotypical images that people have assimilated from textbooks, movies, and television. In some cases, Indian people may indeed produce these dolls. In most cases, however, they represent an appropriation of Native identity by non-Natives. Even Barbie now comes in a Native American version.

In at least one case in the early twentieth century, however, potters at Cochiti Pueblo in New Mexico pulled a reverse appropriation in ceramic figures that they made for the burgeoning tourist trade sparked by the Santa Fe Railroad and Fred Harvey's hotels and tours through the Southwest. They often painted the figures to represent the common cowboy attire of fringed leather jackets and cowboy boots worn by tourists. Other figures represented missionary priests. In a clever reversal of meaning, the Cochiti potters appropriated the identities of the outsiders who came to observe them as strange and exotic beings, and they sold that identity back to the tourists, who may not have fully realized the implications of what they were buying.

Dolls can be used to teach Indian children about tribal traditions, ideals, and values. They can also teach non-Native people something about Indian cultures. Certainly details of clothing and regalia can have a kind of ethnographic value. But in a deeper sense, the doll is a universal symbol that makes the "Exotic Other" more familiar. Dolls strike emotional chords with people in ways that draw them into sympathy with different cultures. People can imagine the children who treasured these dolls. They can think about the mothers who made dolls for their children, and about the children who fashioned their own dolls out of corncobs, cornhusks, buckskin, sheep's wool, or scraps of cloth obtained from traders.

The following pages open and illuminate the vision of what dolls represent in Native societies, and that vision can create a bridge between Indian and non-Indian cultures. The universality of dolls is the keystone of that bridge.

—Clara Sue Kidwell

(Choctaw/Chippewa)

Director, Native American Studies Program

University of Oklahoma

FROM THE PAST

ANCIENT DOLL-LIKE FIGURES made of stone, bone, and ivory have been found in archaeological sites all over the world. The earliest, called "Venus" figurines because they represent women with clearly marked sexual features, appear in the Upper Paleolithic period in Europe, more than 25,000 years ago. They are thought to have some connection with human or animal fertility.

Small representations of human figures occur in many early cultures throughout the Americas. They show great variation in form and style and seem to appear at all levels of cultural development, from small hunting-and-gathering societies to the great states of Mesoamerica and Peru. The most ancient ones known so far in the Americas come from Ecuador and are more than 4,000 years old.

For archaeologists, who know how to read the record of the past from the objects people have left behind, the smallest clue can yield information. Plant fragments and animal bones, as well as food-processing equipment, tell about ancient diets. House remains reveal the size and composition of the groups who lived together. Grave goods, or the lack of them, can express social differences: whether some people were richer or more important than others, for example. Implements such as spindle whorls can indicate that people had textiles, whether or not any textile fragments remain. Objects that are foreign, either in material or style, suggest trade with other areas.

Archaeological figurines can be a particularly rich source of information about the people who made them. Unlike tools and utensils shaped for a primarily utilitarian purpose, miniature

Figure 8. Figures of cast gold and silver were reportedly used during the Inka period as ritual offerings and as grave furnishings for high-status persons. They were sometimes dressed in woven ponchos and wore feather headdresses. At least one such figure was found next to a child who had apparently been sacrificed, perhaps as part of a ritual marking the passing of the Solar Year. 5/4120

representations of people are products of the maker's view of humanity and express cultural values. Details chosen to define a human being or a deity reveal ancient customs, ideology, and religious beliefs.

The ways people choose to alter or adorn their own bodies for beauty or high status are also illustrated in their figurines, some of which reflect practices such as head flattening, tooth filing, tattooing, or body painting. Clothing and ornaments on figurines also provide information. A remarkable assemblage of Maya clay figures from the Chiapas/Guatemala area appear to be wearing long *huipiles* (sleeveless blouses) woven of fine cotton gauze with embroidered designs.[1] A figurine from Ecuador, made as a whistle, is shown wearing a skirt with varicolored stripes (figure 9). Small doll figures wear necklaces, earrings, headdresses, and other ornaments, evidence that ancient peoples shared the same aesthetic sense as people today.

Archaeological figures also reveal occupations, roles, and activities. Warriors, priests, musicians, acrobats, dancers, and women weaving at looms are all found among Mexican figurines, for example, and show that activities that are common today were also familiar more than 2,000 years ago. Figures that appear to represent shamans occur throughout the Americas, offering evidence of the widespread antiquity of that role.

The techniques and materials used in making figures can also provide insights. An abundance of hand-modeled dolls suggests that many people were making them, perhaps for their own personal use. If made of cast gold or silver, or carved from jade or other rare, expensive materials, they were more probably the work of full-time craftsmen with special skills. The presence of such craftsmen indicates a society complex and advanced enough to support people who do not produce food and implies that there may have been other kinds of specialists as well. The great uniformity in mold-made figurines may mean an increase in standardization in the sense that not only a great many people used figurines but also that there was a wide consensus on their proper form.

Wear marks can be clues as to how prehistoric figures were used. Some appear to be freshly made and handled hardly at all. Their pristine quality suggests that they may have been made as offerings for the dead. Others show signs of wear and erosion, as if they had been frequently touched or rubbed. The heads or arms may be broken off in certain patterned ways, as if they had been deliberately destroyed. Some figures show wear only on the bottom, as if they had been standing or sitting for a long time in a shrine or on an altar.

The locations in which figures are found can also provide information. In certain prehistoric phases they appear in the ruins of temples, shrines, or ceremonial centers, while at other periods they occur in the remains of domestic dwellings or as part of the household trash, as if they had been discarded after use. Their presence in houses rather than shrines or temples suggests their use as playthings or as part of a local cult, separate from the state religion practiced by the priests and upper classes.

Much remains unknown about the function of archaeological figurines. Many are collected by pothunters to supply the antiquities market, and the removal from cultural context destroys irreplaceable information. We can postulate, however, that ancient doll-like forms were probably used in a variety of ways: as ritual objects, as grave offerings, perhaps as curing figures, and as toys. And if we assume that human behavior of today is like that of the past, any one doll may have served multiple uses, just as the present-day Kuna curing dolls are sold to tourists or handed over to children as toys once their first purpose has been accomplished (see *For Power*).

We do not know whether the earliest hunting and gathering peoples in the Western Hemisphere made human effigies, for their cultural remains consist almost entirely of stone tools and projectile points. We do know that some time during the period called Archaic, which began about 10,000 years ago, people began burying their dead with exotic and beautiful grave goods such as shaped stone axes. In northeastern North America, burial pits were lined with red hematite, a substance that may have represented the color of life. Human effigies are rare for the Archaic period. A 4,000-year-old Red Paint cemetery at Port au Choix, in Newfoundland, however, suggests that effigies may have been more plentiful than the archaeological record indicates.[2] Located on an abandoned beach near the Gulf of St. Lawrence, the cemetery is thick with tiny shell fragments that have helped to neutralize the normal acidity of the soil and thus preserved materials that would decompose under most other conditions. This natural action has allowed preservation of objects made of animal bone and antler, including small human and animal figurines. We do not know what function these figurines served for the living, but their presence in graves along with other objects thought to have had a magico-religious purpose suggests that they may have been intended to serve some role in the afterlife.

Like the Archaic hunters and gatherers, the ancient Eskimo people also had small, sturdy, and easily carried fetishes representing both animals and persons. Archaeological evidence indicates that such fetishes, often made of walrus ivory, have been part of Eskimo life for at least 2,000 years. They may have been used both for hunting magic and personal protection from misfortune, as they

Figure 10. This tiny wooden doll, excavated from a trash heap, may have been a lost or discarded toy. It appears to be a man wearing boots and fur trousers. *18/2998*

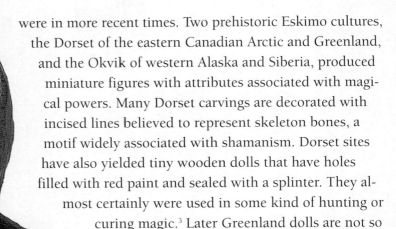

were in more recent times. Two prehistoric Eskimo cultures, the Dorset of the eastern Canadian Arctic and Greenland, and the Okvik of western Alaska and Siberia, produced miniature figures with attributes associated with magical powers. Many Dorset carvings are decorated with incised lines believed to represent skeleton bones, a motif widely associated with shamanism. Dorset sites have also yielded tiny wooden dolls that have holes filled with red paint and sealed with a splinter. They almost certainly were used in some kind of hunting or curing magic.[3] Later Greenland dolls are not so clearly meant for ritual use and may well have been toys (figure 10).

Interpretations of archaeological material can be broadened by observing recent ethnographic use, especially when there is a fairly close relation in time between the two. In historic times, tiny ivory figures were sewn to clothing or worn on a string around the neck as personal amulets. One Siberian shaman was reported to have many small dolls sewn to the coat he wore when treating the sick. These practices, possibly continued from the prehistoric period, may explain small figures found in archaeological sites, many of which have what appear to be holes for suspension.

Eskimo archaeological sites are also filled with headless ivory dolls. Although they may have been broken in children's play, the large number suggests that the breakage was deliberate. Well into the twentieth century, on St. Lawrence Island there was a custom of breaking dolls when a child died. Likewise, when a shaman died, the dolls he used in curing were broken in the same manner. Froelich Rainey, an archaeologist who worked on St. Lawrence Island, associated the broken dolls with contemporary ceremonies, citing the practice of making small wooden figures, feeding them with blubber during the ritual, and then burning them.

In another example, Zena Pearlstone Mathews discusses certain Iroquoian figures of bone or antler from sites dated at approximately A.D. 1550 to 1660.[4] A number of these figures have the arms placed in a "position of modesty," one hand over the chest and the other covering the genitals. It was commonly assumed that they represented a "shy female covering herself" and were made in response to the diffusion of Jesuit missionary ideas. Mathews argues that most of the figures actually show neither male nor female sexual features. One or two seem to be wearing caps or headdresses depicting horns like those worn by shamans. The figures found in burials are nearly always associated with children and adolescents; one cache of five was found with an infant.

Ethnographic evidence offers two pieces of information helpful in interpreting these figures. First, the Seneca reported half a century ago that, "their ancestors used bone images in the practice of witchcraft." Secondly, Mathews refers to a 1909 report describing a photograph of a dead child in its coffin. Sewed to the picture frame were dozens of tiny figures carved from date pits. They were said to be mythic dwarfs who appeared in dreams and promised aid and protection if images of them were made and cared for. Briefly, Mathews' conclusion is that these small figures were not only used in witchcraft but also placed in graves to protect the souls of children from witches. The position of the hands remains a mystery but Mathews suggests that it may express supernatural power rather than modesty.

Hunting and gathering was the predominant way of life in North America for thousands of years. But by about 1500 B.C., the Adena people of the Ohio Valley region had begun to develop agriculture and pottery as well as to construct the large earthworks and burial mounds that excited the imagination of nineteenth-century antiquarians.

By 300 B.C. in this area, the Hopewell culture had emerged. "Hopewell" may actually have been a religious cult that spread rapidly from one local group to another. Some Hopewell burial mounds contained hundreds of individuals and show evidence of great social differentiation. People of high status were provided with rich offerings of freshwater pearls, as well as Great Lakes copper, conch shells from the Gulf Coast, and grizzly bear teeth from the Rocky Mountains, evidence of widespread trading networks.

A few of the figurines of this period were made in a highly naturalistic style. At the Turner Mound in Ohio, a group of figures had

Figure 11. Unearthed at a site on the Wabash River in Indiana, this clay figure resembles a baby wrapped in swaddling clothes. Small figures strapped to a board have been found in the American Southwest as well as Mesoamerica, and have been interpreted as baby-doll toys as well as ritual objects. *5/6396*

been placed on an altar at the center of the mound.[5] They were carefully hand-modeled to represent different individuals with distinctive clothing and hairstyles. Both men and women were portrayed, including one man who may have been a warrior and a kneeling figure believed to be a shaman. The largest figure depicts a man with his hands crossed over his abdomen. It is postulated that it represented a corpse and that the other figures may have been arranged around it to represent a mortuary group. Perhaps the scene, resting at the heart of a large earthen mound, was intended to commemorate the death of a powerful leader.

Following the Hopewell, the prehistoric phase called Mississippian flourished from A.D. 1000 to the arrival of the Spanish in 1539. Mississippian culture may have been a northern variation of a culture complex from Mesoamerica, typified by fortified towns and giant, flat-topped temple mounds. These towns are generally considered chiefdoms, societies controlled by a single, powerful hereditary ruler.

The human effigies from this period are small statues carved of stone or wood, often in male/female pairs. They were placed in charnel houses, buildings where the dead were reverently laid out. John White, the English artist who accompanied Sir Walter Raleigh to the Carolinas in 1585, saw and sketched one of these houses, the bodies of the dead guarded by a seated figure carved of stone or wood.[6] It has been suggested that the effigies represented ancestor figures, perhaps the founders of the chief's lineage or a clan. If so, the Mississippian effigy figures may indicate a change in the direction of civic monuments. Unlike the Hopewell figurines, made to be hidden away in a burial mound for only the gods to see, the Mississippian effigies may themselves have represented a kind of public monument—perhaps a reminder of the importance of the chief's lineage.

Smaller doll-like forms, possibly for individual use, are also found in Mississippian sites. One tiny clay figure, washed out of a river bank in Indiana, seems to depict an infant swaddled in a blanket or some other wrapping (figure 11). Similar pieces from prehistoric sites in the American Southwest have been interpreted both as fertility figures and as toy babies, but the function of this one is unknown.

Small clay figurines are widely distributed throughout the Southwest, though they are few in number in comparison with the thousands from Mexico. The earliest date from approximately A.D. 300 at a Mogollon site in eastern Arizona. Noel Morss, who studied southwestern figurines, classified them into a Northern Tradition (Utah, Colorado, and northern Arizona) and a Southern Tradition (southern Arizona and New Mexico). Most of the Northern Tradition figurines were made about A.D. 1000 during a brief period when climactic changes allowed for some development of agriculture and settled life. Of unfired pottery, these figures with small arms and legs depict both men and women, the women wearing tiny skirts made of rolled bands of clay. Traces of red and blue paint remain on some of the figures.

One particular group from a cave in northern Utah consists of six female and five male figures. They are more elaborate than any other known figurines of the Northern Tradition, dressed in short aprons or breechcloths, necklaces, earrings, and pendants, all rendered in clay. The general similarity in appearance, the fact that they were found in a single cache, and some idiosyncrasies such as the tendency to make the left eye-slit a little longer and shallower than the right, all led Morss to postulate that they were from the hand of a single individual. He thought that they were made at different times, however, for the color of the clay and the paints used in decoration vary. He also argued that they were intended to be male/female pairs, with one male figure being lost or broken at some time in the past.

Morss viewed the northern Utah doll forms as fertility figures involving "concepts basically unchanged since Paleolithic times."[7] Most fertility figurines throughout the world represent females. There is evidence, however, that in California and the Southwest during the historic period, both male and female dolls served as fertility amulets, depending on whether a woman wanted a boy or girl baby. If the figures Morss studied are indeed pairs, such a practice may be many hundreds of years old.

Morss discusses another type of figurine, the "babe in cradle," widely distributed not only in the Southwest but also in Ecuador, Mexico, and as far north as Tennessee. "Babes in cradles" depict small human figures lying on the back, fastened to a bed or a cradleboard by a binding across the upper part of the body. The term is something of a misnomer, for some of the "babes" clearly resemble adults, and many of the "cradles" are actually beds with frames and feet. Various interpretations of these figures identify

Figure 12. Figures of nude young women with long hair are the earliest type found at the Formative site of Tlatilco, near Mexico City. The eyes are formed by large holes surrounded by a circle of tiny dots, and the arms are held close to the body. The hands-to-chin stance may have an erotic meaning. *22/708*

them as baby-doll toys, images of persons engaged in ritual drug-taking, and depictions of women confined during menstruation or giving birth; probably no one explanation covers all examples.

Almost all the archaeological figurines of the Southwest are made of clay or stone, but one carved of wood may be a precursor of a katsina doll. It is a painted figure from Double Butte cave in southern Arizona, dated at about the twelfth or thirteenth century.[8] The head appears to be masked, and two painted diagonal lines across the chest suggest a bandolier shoulder belt, worn by some katsina dancers today. Hopi legends say that the katsinas came originally from Casa Grande, near the cave site.

Handmade figurines of clay, mostly females, survive in great numbers from the Hohokam culture of Arizona. Thousands of ancient figurines have also been found in Mexico and Central America, in some archaeological sites the number of figurines and fragments almost equaling the number of pieces of broken bowls and vessels. Figurines are found in the ruins of temples and domestic dwellings, in tombs, and on trash heaps. They show so many styles and belong to so many cultural traditions that we here focus on only a few examples whose form and context reveal information about ancient lifeways in Mesoamerica.

One of the largest groups of Mesoamerican figurines was produced during a period known to archaeologists as the Formative, or Preclassic. This span of time, from approximately 2500 B.C. to A.D. 1, saw the establishment of agriculture and village life, population growth, and the invention of pottery. Some village settlements eventually became larger and wealthier than others, and there was increasingly complex social organization and the development of interregional trade networks.

The Formative site of Tlatilco, near present-day Mexico City, has yielded thousands of hand-modeled figurines. The earliest Tlatilco figures, possibly the earliest in central Mexico, depict slender, nude young women with long hair and punctuate eyes (figure 12). There are many other kinds; mothers with children, women with dishes of food, masked and costumed dancers, ball players, and musicians. The vast majority represent women, and may be fertility figurines, but this interpretation does not explain the male figures, nor the ordinary everyday activities depicted. A few have been found in graves, and one theory is that they were intended to be attendants of some kind, like the Tang dynasty tomb figures of China.

Female figures worldwide are often interpreted as belonging to an agricultural fertility cult, symbolizing the fecundity of Mother Earth. In the Old World, such female figures are found in the grain-growing areas of the Mediterranean, India, and the Middle East, and it is argued that the early maize growers of Mesoamerica made similar connections between human and agricultural fertility. At a later period, the Aztecs were said to place small figurines in their planted fields to ensure a good harvest, and in some places in Mexico today farmers still leave small figures in their fields for the same reason.

Many of the Formative female figurines share a number of features that archaeologists have used to designate them as "pretty ladies." They are indeed "pretty," sleek and plump, carefully modeled

Figure 13. Thousands of these hand-modeled female figures have been found throughout southern Guanajuato and Michoacán, Mexico. Almost all are nude women crowned with elaborate headdresses and adorned with necklaces, earspools, and bracelets made of bits of clay. Some of them, such as this one, are pregnant. They seem to have been intended only as offerings, for few of them are made to stand and the backs are roughly finished. *23/8701*

Figure 14. This Colima female figure wears a tiny tasseled apron, and painted designs cover her body. Such figures have been found in deep-shaft tombs in West Mexico, often collected in groups and stored in jars. Possibly they served as attendants of the dead, accompanying the soul into the next world. *23/5505*

to display large breasts, and fat thighs and buttocks. Their hair is often elaborately arranged and adorned with ornaments and headdresses. Many are nude or dressed only in a small skirt or apron. They wear necklaces and earrings, breast ornaments, or body paint (figures 13, 14, 15, and 16). A considerable number of them are overtly erotic: the genitalia are clearly defined; and frequently they sit in a spread-legged position and are shown making sexual or erotic gestures, with a hand on the chin, cheeks, thighs, belly, breast, or genitals.

Anna Roosevelt has suggested that rather than representing agricultural goddesses, the "pretty ladies" may have been part of a cult to encourage human reproduction.[9] Roosevelt points out that women who are plump and well nourished are likely to bear more and healthier children. People in many cultures consider plumpness a sign of beauty and femininity. If the "pretty ladies" represent the female ideal, their presence in such large numbers during the Formative period may indicate an ideology that emphasized population increase and placed special value on women's reproductive role. Roosevelt points out that the hypothesis can be tested by the analysis of the health status of skeletons in prehistoric burials.

"Pretty ladies" are sometimes found in graves, and the majority of those seem to be buried with females. Most of them occur in household remains, however, as if they were part of the everyday life of ordinary people. This occurrence may still be compatible with their use in a cult of female fertility, for domestic areas were more likely to be the domain of women than of men, whose rituals typically took place in temples and their environs.

A number of the figures appear to depict pregnant women or those who have borne children; Warren Barbour has pointed out in his study of figurines from Teotihuacan that some have folds in the midriff as women do after pregnancy.[10] Gerardo Reichel-Dolmatoff suggests that these figures may have been used not to induce fertility but to protect women from complications during pregnancy and childbirth. He states that present-day Colombian Indian men concern themselves not with a wife's becoming pregnant but with her continued health during pregnancy and delivery.[11]

The Formative period also saw the development of what is generally considered to be the first Mesoamerican civilization, the Olmec culture, centered in the Gulf Coast region of Vera Cruz and Tabasco. The Olmec thrived from about 1500–400 B.C. They built

Figure 15. This finely modeled Playa de los Muertos figure from Belize portrays a plump, seated woman, her elbow resting on a jar. She wears a small skirt as well as a cap, and her teeth may have been filed to enhance her beauty. *4/3872*

Figure 16. Another kind of figure from Nayarit is also found in the shaft tombs of West Mexico. They are called "Chinesco," a name bestowed by antiquities dealers for what was considered to be an Asian appearance. The spread-legged pose, the plump thighs, and the baby held in the crook of the arm all suggest that this figure may have been used in a cult of fertility. *23/7665*

Figure 17. Excavated at the Olmec site of La Venta in southern Vera Cruz was this puzzling find: 16 figures of jade, granite, and serpentine, deliberately arranged to form a scene. One stands, back against a basalt column, while four figures appear to be "passing in review" and others stand back as observers. The scene has been variously interpreted as priests performing a ritual, dancers, or candidates for some sacrifice. Whatever its meaning, it may replicate an actual event, for the central courtyard of the ceremonial center of La Venta is marked by a palisade of large basalt columns similar in appearance to the miniature ones included here. Photograph by Michel Zabé. Courtesy of the National Museum of Anthropology, Mexico City.

ceremonial centers and are thought to have originated certain religious beliefs and a ritual calendar that are also found in later Mesoamerican civilizations such as the Maya and the Aztec. The Olmec are also considered the first to bring forth an elite class with rulers identified with deities.

Although lowland Olmec habitation sites have small clay female figures, most Olmec art was identified with the elite culture and was associated with ritual activity and sumptuous grave goods for the upper class. The doll-like forms produced for this elite culture are quite different from the "pretty ladies" made and used by ordinary people. They include figures carved of jade and stone as well as hollow dolls of clay. Many have been interpreted as jaguar-men or fat babies, sometimes with their hands to their heads. Some are dwarfs or hunchbacks; some are old women carrying babies with jaguar features.

The meaning of these mysterious images is still in question. They have been called sky gods, rain gods, and beings born from the union of a woman and a jaguar, but the iconography is not well understood. It does seem clear, however, that the doll-like figures of the Olmec were not intended for mundane, domestic use, but refer in some way to myths and a complex ritual activity carried on by religious specialists. The "pretty ladies" belong to everyday life; the Olmec figures express a cosmology concerned with justifying a religion of priests and statesmen.

Much of the wealth found in the Olmec ceremonial centers was received in trade or tribute from other parts of Mexico and seems to have been intended solely as grave goods for high-ranking persons. It does not turn up in ordinary contexts. There were probably provincial trading centers throughout Mexico: for example, the center at Las Bocas, in Puebla, where Olmec-style figurines like the one in figure 18 have been found. Whether such objects were gifts to a local ruler or whether Olmec people from Vera Cruz colonized places like Las Bocas is not yet known.

Figure 18. This Olmec-style ceramic figure was found at Las Bocas, a highland center located along the trade route to Guerrero, Mexico. Many Olmecoid objects have been found far from the Olmec heartland. We do not yet know whether this wide distribution resulted from extensive trade, colonization, or imitation of Olmec luxury items by provincial people, but if figures like this one were ritual objects, their presence may indicate spread of an entire complex of religious imagery. *23/5495*

Figure 19. This small clay Valdivia figure is more than 4,000 years old. It is one of many female dolls, all nude with distinctive hairstyles. They seem to have been casually discarded in household trash and may have been made by women for a specific purpose and then thrown away. Their nudity and phallic head form suggest use in a cult of human fertility. *24/8401*

Formative "pretty ladies" also occur in South America, both in the tropical lowlands east of the Andes and in coastal Ecuador. Roosevelt characterizes the Formative tropical lowland cultures as areas of incipient maize cultivation and rapidly expanding population; she postulates that the "pretty ladies" express a "populationist" ideology, understandable where a larger population was needed for food production and warfare. The site of Valdivia in coastal Ecuador was a fishing-farming village in Formative times, a place with a food supply rich enough to support sedentary village life. By 2500 B.C. at Valdivia, crude stone figurines appear, barely recognizable as human shapes, having only a simple groove to indicate the legs. But by 2300 B.C. more elaborate clay figures were being produced. Most have tiny faces almost hidden by great masses of hair modeled in a variety of styles. A few are pregnant or carrying a baby; some are two-headed; and there are even a few males wearing a belt-and-loincloth arrangement still worn today in the tropical forests of South America.

Like the Formative figurines of Mesoamerica, those from Valdivia are usually found in household trash, as if they had been casually discarded. Also, like the Mesoamerican figures, several possible uses for them have been suggested, including toys, fertility figures, and curing figures used by shamans and thrown away after they have done their work. Betty Meggers and Clifford Evans discount their use in a cult of fertility, saying that only a few are pregnant and that genitalia are not shown.[12] However, most of the figurines have well-defined breasts, and Donald Lathrap argues that the whole shape is explicitly phallic, the massed hair being analogous to the glans.[13] If the figures are in fact symbolic representations of male/female union, they may well have been made to encourage fertility.

Figure 20. This mold-made Mexican marionette dating from about A.D. 500 is a masterpiece of the potter's art. The scroll designs in low relief typify the Vera Cruz style, but are more usually found on stone yokes and other objects associated with a ritual ball game. The function of this doll is unknown; possibly, movable figures were used in divination or to perform magical tricks. *23/735*

Lathrap also offers evidence for their possible use by shamans. He points out that some are found in association with miniature clay copies of the wooden seats used by shamans today throughout the tropical forest cultures of South America. Contemporary shamans also use hallucinogenic drugs to produce visions, drugs that are often ground on a palette and ingested through a snuff tube. At least two of the Valdivia figurines have the top of the head shaped into a small, flat snuff dish of the type found throughout South America from Chile to the Caribbean. The association of shamanism with curing stools, palettes, and figurines is widespread and could well have been in existence in Ecuador 4,000 years ago, at the dawn of settled agricultural life.

With the building of the great city of Teotihuacan around the time of Christ, a new kind of doll form developed—figures mass-produced in specialized workshops by means of molds. By the Classic period in Mesoamerica (A.D. 300–900), society had grown enough in size and complexity to support such specialization, and there is evidence that artisans working full-time at their crafts produced not only figurines but also other pottery objects, obsidian pieces, and metalwork.

Barbour's study of the Classic period Teotihuacan figurines and the workshops that produced them indicates that they seem to have been made predominantly for everyday use. Few are found in burials, the majority appearing in the remains of houses. Some from temple ruins appear to represent deities. One rare type, from the upper part of the Pyramid of the Sun, shows a naturalistic figure with a were-jaguar mouth. Other figurines from the same area include a few wearing headdresses associated with the Fire God and what may be a Teotihuacan version of the later Aztec flayed god Xipe-Totec. There seem to be an equal number of male and female figures at Teotihuacan, suggesting that they no longer relate to a woman's cult of human fertility but instead express a new kind of complex religious belief.

One type of figurine found in graves as well as house remains is the jointed puppet. These figures have been identified both as males and as sexless beings, but Barbour argues that they are females who have borne children. He suggests that the movable limbs of these puppets may have been manipulated, perhaps by shamans, to ensure a successful and easy childbirth. A woman who died in childbirth might be buried with her puppet as a talisman.

The Classic period Vera Cruz version of the puppet in figure 20 appears to represent a male adorned with the low-relief scroll designs also found on ceremonial stone objects of the period. We do not know how such puppets were used, but Stephan de Borhegyi refers to a Mexican legend of the destruction of the Toltecs by means of a small figure that is made to dance on the hand of a sorcerer.[14] If the Toltecs were not familiar with stringed puppets, such manipulation of a figure must have caused wonder and fright, and it may have become a legend remembered over time.

The Classic period civilization of the Maya is known for advanced architecture and art, hieroglyphic writing, a highly developed calendar based on a sophisticated knowledge of astronomy, an esoteric religious system with a pantheon of gods, and a great interest in the genealogy and activities of rulers. Classic Mayas produced many doll-like forms, which reflect an elite culture. Rather than representing nude females intended for use by ordinary people, Maya figures depict either deities or upper-class individuals elaborately dressed and adorned. Many are found as grave offerings for the nobility, such as those from Jaina Island off the coast of Campeche, Mexico. These delicately modeled polychromed figures, some of which are also whistles or rattles, portray elegantly dressed dignitaries, warriors, priests, and women who may be priestesses or deities in human form. The women are no longer young and pretty, but matronly and dignified, and they are sometimes engaged in activities pertaining to solemn religious ritual. The woman in figure 21 has drops of blood on her cheeks and chin, a sign that she has just performed a ritual of self-sacrifice by passing thorns through her tongue. Such cults were part of the upper-class Maya world and separated the nobility from the everyday life of the common people.

In the Late Classic Maya site of Lagartero, in Chiapas, one type of mold-made figurine is found in refuse deposits. More than half of the figures represent females, elegantly dressed in what appears to be fine embroidered cotton. They may be part of a religious cult practiced by women. Archaeologist Susanna Ekholm suggests that they may have been made for a special event, such as a ceremony marking the end of a calendrical cycle.[15] Like the Jaina figurines, they seem to indicate that women had important roles in elite religious practices.

Figure 21. This dignified and regal Maya figurine from Mexico is an upper-class matron of substantial years. Indications of her elite status are the elaborate headdress, the intentionally flattened forehead, and the round ornament on her forehead, a sign of high rank and beauty. The dots on her cheeks and chin represent drops of blood and indicate that she has just participated in a ritual of self-sacrifice by passing thorns through her tongue. Such ritual bloodletting was practiced ceremonially by the Maya upper classes. *23/2274*

The Aztec Empire flourished in the Valley of Mexico during the Post-classic period from about A.D. 1200 to the arrival of the Spanish in 1519. Spanish chronicles tell us that each city-state had its own patron deity or spirit that personified aspects of nature. They also report that the Aztecs had great numbers of "idols," or *idolillos*, which were seen by the Spanish priests as heathen images. There were indeed a great many religious figures, made both of permanent

Figure 22. This Aztec woman, wearing earspools and a brocaded skirt, shows none of the earthiness associated with fertility figurines. She may represent a goddess or a woman of the upper class. *1/2238*

Figure 23. Mold-made figures of women, some holding babies, appear in the central Andes by A.D. 800. Many wear head shawls but others such as this Moche one from Peru have long braids. They seem to be associated with women and children, for they are found in children's graves as well as in the remains of houses. They may have been favorite toys. *15/7679*

Figure 24. Casas Grandes, in Chihuahua, Mexico, was a trading center for goods moving north and south between Mesoamerica and North America. This little figure, actually a ceramic jar, shows style similarities to ancient pottery of the American Southwest. *11/9878*

materials like clay and stone and perishable substances such as wood. Images of one god were made from *tzoalli*, a dough of amaranth seeds, maize, and honey.[16] Images were set up in temples, in open-air shrines, in cultivated fields, or near sacred trees. Each house was reported to have an inside altar with images of household gods placed on it. Farmers strung figurines on cords stretched over the cornfields, perhaps to serve not only for the spiritual protection of the crops but also for the practical purpose of frightening away the birds. Merchants carried cult images with them when they went on long journeys and set them up each night when they stopped to sleep. Some of these figures were thrown away at the time of the New Fire Ceremony and replaced with new ones. Some images, such as one known as the Goddess with the Temple Headdress, appear to have been mass-produced, possibly for sale in the markets.

It appears that the common people venerated the deities associated with agricultural fertility, while the ruling classes worshipped creator gods associated with war and sacrifice and the powers of destruction. Most of these ruling class deities were male, and many appear as armed warriors of terrifying aspect. The figurines of women, dignified rather than erotic, may refer not to human fertility but rather to some more austere expression of religious belief (figure 22).

In contrast with Mesoamerica, where most of the Classic period figurines seem to be connected with an esoteric religious complex, those of Peru appear to have been made predominantly as children's toys. In her study of Peruvian figurines, Rose Solecki argues that most of the figurines have characteristics still common to dolls today: they are nude (that is, their bodies are not adorned with elaborate ornaments or paint); the sex is indicated but not exaggerated; they are sturdy and easy to handle; and most depict either women or female children.[17] The majority are simple standing figures, although a few carry babies, play musical instruments, or carry objects such as household goods.

The Peruvian dolls are found in both household refuse and in graves, but only in the graves of women and children. Not every child's or woman's grave has them, and Solecki suggests that it may have been an individual choice whether or not to place a favorite toy in a grave as an offering. The small, mold-made Moche doll in figure 23 seems to conform to Solecki's description of a toy. Sturdy and easy to hold, it represents a woman carrying a baby. The Chancay doll in figure 25 seems to have been a little too large for a child to manipulate with ease, although Solecki points out that even today some dolls are made in very large sizes. Smaller versions of this one were also made, some dressed in cloth ponchos.

The reed and fabric dolls found in Chancay graves may not have been made for play but rather as attendants to the dead, for some of them seem to have shamanic significance. Other dolls presumably made for ritual purposes are the figures of cast gold and silver used as grave offerings (figure 8). One such figure, found in Chile and dressed in a fabric poncho and feather headdress, was found in the grave of a young child who had been sacrificed, perhaps as an offering to the sun at the beginning of the solar year.[18]

Archaeological doll forms seem, then, to have served a variety of purposes. Those small and portable dolls made by hunting and gathering peoples apparently were used as personal amulets, perhaps to bring good fortune or protection from evil. In sedentary agricultural areas, dolls were evidently used as devices to bring earthly fertility and perhaps also to aid human reproduction and health. In more complex, stratified societies, doll forms seemingly served to depict deities or to carry out rituals related to a state religious cosmology. In addition, dolls everywhere may have been made for that most venerable of purposes, as toys.

Figure 25. This large hollow female figure from the Chancay Valley in Peru dates from A.D. 1000 to 1500. She wears a painted-on square cap with a decorated headband. Figures like this one, but smaller, have been found with clothing or with clothes painted on and may have been toys, although the large size of this one suggests other possible uses for it. *24/9499*

FOR PLAYING

Figure 26. A Plains play camp of the 19th century might have several toy tipis such as these, arranged in a circle and enhanced with toy dolls, cradleboards, horses, and miniature equipment. Men or occasionally women painted full-sized tipis with designs showing scenes of battle and war exploits of the painter or a male relative. The miniature tipi in the foreground shows a battle in progress, with the horses' tails tied up as they would be for war. The man and bear painted on the door flap may refer to some ritual activity. The man, who wears a long hair ornament made of German-silver hair plates, may be the father or uncle of the little girl who owned this tipi. *2/9535*, 12/2242, 22/4820, 8836, 2/1535

ACCORDING TO MAX VON BOEHN, author of the first scholarly work on dolls and puppets, "The doll existed for thousands of years before the first child took possession of it."[1] Boehn was convinced that the earliest representations of human figures were made as religious objects and that toys came much later. Perhaps, he suggests, fertility figures were passed on to children after they had served their ritual purpose, and these figures may have been the precursor of dolls made especially for children. Since von Boehn's time, research in sociobiology has indicated that the need to cuddle, nurture, and love may be part of our biological makeup. If true, we can postulate that play dolls were inherent to human activity from the very beginning, and may have preceded figures used in ritual.

Toy dolls may not necessarily be recognizable as such, either in archaeological sites or in undocumented collections of ethnographic objects. Observers of children know that, for a child, anything can become a doll—a stick, a leaf, a bit of ragged cloth, a peculiarly shaped stone, a corncob. William L. White's account of a World War II refugee child from the London blitz, *A Journey for Margaret*, tells of a little girl's devotion to a shell casing that she wrapped in a blanket and carried with her everywhere.[2]

Probably dolls have always been made of both perishable and permanent materials. Eskimo children make dolls of scraps of sealskin tied with thongs at the "waist" and "neck." Bororo children of Brazil construct dolls of palm leaf fiber. Children in the corn-growing

A cheife Heroroans wyfe of Pomeoc.
and her daughter of the age of .8. or.
.10. yeares.

Figure 27. English artist John White sketched this little Sacaton girl from 16th-century Virginia. She carries a wooden doll dressed in Elizabethan clothing, probably a gift from one of the colonists. Reproduced by courtesy of the Trustees of the British Museum.

areas of the Americas play with dolls made of corncobs or husks. Few of these dolls survive very long. Like the hollyhock dolls of rural North American children, they can be quickly created for an hour or a day of play, and as quickly discarded. Many of them, without the benefit of a child's vivid imagination, might not even be recognizable as dolls.

Dolls made of sturdier stuff have survived, however, along with reports by early visitors to the Americas who took notice of children's activities. When Sir Walter Raleigh visited the English settlement in the Virginia of 1585, he brought with him gifts of wooden dolls of the type called Flanders babies for the children of the settlers—and perhaps for the Indian children as well. John White, the artist who accompanied Raleigh, sketched a little Sacaton girl happily brandishing an unmistakably Elizabethan doll. White wrote that the children were "greatlye dilighted with puppetts, and babes which were brought oute of England"[3] (figure 27). It seems clear that such dolls were instantly recognizable as children's playthings.

Beneath the delights of doll play is a more serious adult purpose: teaching children the skills that will be required when they grow up. By imitating their mothers, little girls learn how to feed, dress, and care for a baby. They observe how a baby should be carried, whether in a cradleboard, or slung into a shawl, or astride the hip, and they imitate the culturally prescribed body language of a woman's behavior. They also learn the technical skills needed to make clothes for the family, an art that is for the most part a woman's responsibility.

In the past, when everything was made by hand, children began very young, often by working alongside their mothers or grandmothers, to learn how to scrape and tan hides, spin thread and weave it into cloth, or sew boots with animal sinew. Much practice was required to transform a raw deerskin or a handful of cotton or a bunch of cedar bark into a neatly finished garment. Making doll clothes was a way to learn these essential skills. It was also a means of developing artistic sensibilities.

Even today, when many clothes are bought at the store, children still learn some traditional skills. In many contemporary Native American cultures women expend great energy to construct clothing that is not only well made but also beautiful. Women take pride in the creation of a man's finely quilled shirt or embroidered moccasins,

Figure 28. Two little Yup'ik Eskimo girls carry their dolls in Nome, Alaska, in the early 1930s. Photo by Dr. Leuman M. Waugh. P30045

a boy's colorfully woven poncho, a girl's fur parka trimmed with beads and lace. When a little girl adds, with clumsy stitches, the first beads to a doll's dress, she begins a journey that will culminate with her becoming an accomplished woman, one who brings pride to her family and honor to her husband.

Because children's toy dolls are made of locally available materials, they range from ivory and bone to beeswax and cedar bark. And because they are made within a specific cultural tradition—Seminole dolls, for example, look quite different from Aymara dolls—they mirror in miniature the great stylistic diversity of the Native peoples of the Americas.

The Arctic

For more than 2,000 years, the Eskimo (Inuit) people have lived in the harshest environment in North America, a land of long, dark, bitter cold winters and brief summers. Their survival has been made possible by a series of remarkable inventions—tailored fur clothing (which dates from the Ice Age), the kayak and harpoon to hunt sea mammals, and the dogsled for travel over the Arctic tundra. Eskimo culture, despite its difficulties and discomforts, is enriched by song and dance, by games and stories, and by a warm, close family life.

From Siberia to Greenland, dolls were, and are today, favorite toys of Native children. Nowadays most dolls are store-bought, but in the old days loving fathers carved them from bone or walrus ivory. A few were made of wood, especially along the coasts of Alaska and Greenland where driftwood could be collected on the shore. Each little girl had several, some only an inch high and others perhaps a foot tall. Boys also played with dolls, little half-figures seated in miniature skin kayaks outfitted with small harpoons, paddles, and bladder floats (figure 29).

A Yup'ik Eskimo story from Hooper Bay, Alaska, tells about a doll made of blubber. It concerns Ooloo, a young girl forbidden to marry the man of her choice, so she refused all other suitors. After a while her angry father threw a piece of blubber at her, saying, "Marry that!" Ooloo carved a boy doll from the frozen blubber and dressed it in doll clothes she had made herself. The blubber doll changed into a handsome young man, who married Ooloo, and they were very happy together. But when the warm spring came the Blubber boy melted away "into the floor of his kayak." Ooloo did not mind, for she knew that when winter came she could create a new Blubber boy, dress him in doll clothes, and wish him back to her.[4]

Arctic dolls were apparently made in very large numbers. Vitus Bering visited the coast of Alaska in 1741, Captain James Cook in 1778, and each collected a "good many" dolls dressed in miniature fur clothing.[5] A hundred years later, Edward Nelson, visiting the Bering Strait area for the Smithsonian Institution, reported that: "While making a visit to Sledge Island, two little girls in the house where we stopped amused us by watching their opportunity, while we were busy about other things, to place their dolls standing in a semicircle before us on the floor, while they sat quietly behind as though permitting their dolls to take a look at the strangers."[6]

Figure 29. Eskimo boys played with dolls in toy kayaks outfitted with miniature hunting equipment. This one is from the east coast of Greenland. *19/6279*

Figure 30. A man fishing from a kayak. Mackenzie Delta, Northwest Territory, Canada. Photograph by Donald A. Cadzow, ca. 1918. *N2018*

Those dolls were probably much like the ivory-headed dolls shown in figure 31, with carefully etched features, including eyebrows and, for women, tattoo marks on the chin. In some parts of Alaska, girl dolls were made with frowning mouths and boys with smiling ones, but the only explanation seems to be that they have always been done this way. Some boy dolls had tiny beads placed below the corners of the mouth to represent labrets, the lip plugs worn by Eskimo men. Miniature ivory or bead earrings, nose ornaments, and bracelets or necklaces were often added.

Many dolls were carved without arms, perhaps because that style made them easier to dress and undress. Dolls frequently had several changes of clothing. Miniature parkas were constructed of the skins of small animals, sometimes with the creature's legs becoming the arms of the doll. Little girls on St. Lawrence Island were reported to be always on the lookout for mice, lemmings, and Arctic squirrels that they trapped and skinned to make doll clothes.

Some dolls were made with a wood or ivory torso and legs of soft cloth or stuffed sealskin. They could be made to sit or be carried astride their little mother's back, just like real babies. The ivory torsos found in archaeological sites may have been part of such dolls.

The clothing, hairstyles, and facial decoration on dolls reflect the regional variation found throughout the Arctic. Greenland women, for example, tie their hair up in a topknot and wear thigh-high boots and short trousers, which are quite different from the long parkas worn in the central Arctic.

Children had a full range of miniature accessories for their dolls: seal oil lamps made of clay or soapstone, sleeping mats of fur or grass, sealskin boots and mittens, dishes and bowls carved of wood. Dolls and their gear were stored away in bags made of walrus intestine when not in use.

Wooden dolls carved with great ingenuity were made in Alaska in the area between the Yukon and the Kuskokwim Rivers. The heads are fitted on a wooden pin and attached to strings running the length of the body. Depending on which string is pulled, the doll can be made to turn its head to the right or the left.

Perhaps because many dolls were so realistic, they were sometimes viewed with a kind of ambiguity. Some beliefs and myths about dolls indicate that, for the Eskimo people and their neighbors, even play dolls had about them a certain other-worldliness. Ingalik parents, for example, did not allow their children to take

Figure 31. Little Eskimo girls trapped mice and squirrels to get fur for their doll parkas, and they learned to sew by making doll clothes. The parka on this ivory doll incorporates the legs of an Arctic squirrel for the doll's arms. Tucked inside the parka, in imitation of a mother, is a tiny baby doll. *9/3626*

dolls to bed with them, lest the dolls come alive during the night and bring harm to the child. The rule was apparently not a hard and fast one, however, for if the child cried for the doll, the mother could call for the shaman, or Native doctor, and ask him to perform a ritual to make the doll "safe" to handle.

In southwest Alaska there were restrictions on playing with dolls. Doll play was reserved for the summertime only, outside the house, for if it continued after the coming of the first snow, harm would come to the village. A story of some girls who broke the rule is still fresh in the memory of old people in the village of Chevak. As one of the village elders tells:

"There was a village one time that . . . when they were playing with dolls during the wintertime, the season came about to be spring, and this certain village was still winter, and . . . birds . . . were walking on top of the snow, and they didn't realize that the place around them was summertime, but the village inside was winter."[7]

Still another story, from the lower Yukon, makes a doll responsible for the coming of the winds. In abbreviated form it is told as follows:

> In a village on the lower Yukon lived a man and his wife who had no children. The woman told her husband to go on to the tundra to a solitary tree that grew there and bring back a part of its trunk and make a doll from it.

Figure 32. This wooden doll from Greenland has the elaborate topknot hairstyle worn by Greenland women. She wears a traditional fur-trimmed jacket, high boots, and short pants. *11/3018*

When he returned, he sat down and carved from the wood an image of a small boy, for which his wife made a couple of suits of fur clothing in which she dressed it. The man then carved a set of toy dishes from the wood, and they filled them with food and water and left the doll sitting with the dishes before it. During the night they heard a low whistling sound. They found that the doll had eaten the food and drunk the water, and that its eyes were moving. The delighted woman played with the doll for a long time.

In the morning the doll was gone. They found its tracks following a path of light towards the tree, and then they disappeared. The doll had traveled to the edge of day, where the sky comes down to the earth. He saw that the sky wall was a gutskin that was bulging as if there were a strong force behind it. He cut a hole in the skin with his knife, and a strong wind blew through bringing with it live reindeer. . . . The doll walked all around the edge of the sky wall, making holes with his knife, until he opened the world to all the winds—the southeast wind that brought trees and bushes, the south wind with its rain, the west wind with sleet and spray, and the north wind with its snow and ice. He told all the winds to blow "sometimes hard, sometimes light, and sometimes not at all."

Then he returned to the village, where his parents greeted him with joy. From that time on, parents have made dolls for their children.[8]

Little girls played with dolls until the time of their first menstruation, when they were considered old enough to marry. The importance of doll play in defining childhood was seen in the fact that first menstruation was referred to as "the putting away of dolls." The metaphor is clear. Once a girl is old enough to have babies of her own, she has no further need for the accoutrements of childhood.

Western North America

The people of the Pacific Northwest excel at the art of woodcarving and are famous for their masks, large wooden canoes, and totem poles. Articulated wooden puppets are reserved for ceremonial use (see *For Performance*), and children today play with store-bought dolls. In the past, children's dolls were simple, made of shells, cedar bark, or stones.

Figure 33. The Central Pomoan people of California, among the finest basket-makers in the world, used basketry baby carriers. An early observer wrote that, "a real prize was to have a mother make a little doll-carrying basket that the girl-mother could carry her doll with on her back." This doll, of European origin, has its face darkened with pigment and is wrapped in a piece of quilting. The carrying strap is decorated with beads cut from shell, a type of decoration also used on baskets. *20/7144*

Doll play could become quite elaborate. In the 1940s, old people still recalled how they played "doll house" and acted out stories, using shells for people. A big mussel shell served as a canoe and the little shells set into it made a family, sometimes all of them wearing pointed shell hats. Children used shells for doll dishes also. A round shell might be filled with bits of seaweed to represent a serving dish for a feast, as children imitated their elders at playing "host" and "guest." Children also seized upon bits of cloth to make dolls and to dress up their clamshell dolls. James Swan, who visited the Northwest in 1857, reported, "The girls were very fond of making rag babies and dressing up clamshells like children. One of these girls . . . had a small trunk full of these rag dolls dressed in all sorts of styles, which she used to parade out whenever her friends came to see her."[9]

Tlingit children from Alaska made dolls of beach pebbles, shaping them by resting the pebble on a rock and hitting it with a hammerstone. Children of Vancouver Island had dolls made of shredded cedar bark tied together at the neck, waist, and arms. They resembled somewhat the cornhusk dolls of the Northeast, but were not as carefully made. Some of them were given a wooden cradle or cradleboard, a toy version of the ones their mothers used. Klikitat mothers from Washington made dolls for their little girls out of leather, steaming it into shape and sewing on a leather nose. Yurok children from Oregon and northern California were reported to make dolls from the bluish mud found along rivers and streams. They had miniature cradles for carrying their dolls and were exhorted not to place more than one doll at a time in the cradle because of the Yurok belief that twins bring bad luck.

Most groups in North America and the temperate regions of South America had some kind of cradle into which they strapped a baby for the first few months of its life, and which served as both bed and baby carriage. Styles varied greatly, and materials ranged from birchbark to hide, but virtually everywhere miniature copies of baby carriers were part of doll play.

As Athabaskan and Salish girls played with caribou hide dolls and birchbark baby carriers, Pomoan children of California set their dolls into cradles made of basketry (figure 33). Their cradles were short and scoop-shaped, made of wooden rods sewn together and having a circular hoop to serve as a head protector, a common feature on North American baby carriers. Pomoan children made dolls from wood, from stuffed skins, from clay, and even from wild parsnip tops. One observer reported that the children made the dolls talk to each other. They also took their dolls into the dance house in the center of the village, where they made them dance in imitation of the ceremonial dances of their elders.

Plains

The Great Plains region of North America, extending from Saskatchewan south into Texas, is the home of numerous tribes: the Blackfeet, Crow, Sioux, Arapaho, Cheyenne, and Comanche, among others. In the nineteenth century, buffalo hunting provided food, clothing, and shelter, and warfare was a way to gain glory and honor. Accounts of Plains life at that time make clear that doll play was an integral part of childhood, remembered with pleasure by old people reminiscing about the past. Even today, in the era of commercial dolls, some are still made in the old style, and children play with both kinds.

Plains dolls are made of wood, cloth, or hide. Those made for very young children are extremely simple. A Blackfeet child's first doll might be made by her grandmother, perhaps when they go together to collect firewood. The grandmother chops a section of a birch limb about a foot long. With a knife she cuts a groove about four inches from one end to form the shoulder line, and then whittles a knoblike head with little holes to form the eyes, nose, and mouth. The limb is simply wrapped in a piece of buckskin or cloth to form the clothing.

Agnes Yellow Plume, an Arapaho woman recalling her childhood, describes another simple type of doll, known as the "pieces" doll because it is made of scraps of fabric, or "pieces." She says:

"The dolls we played with were rag dolls. They were merely little round heads with rags hanging down. When we made one, we tried to get a piece of cloth of black-and-white print. The black represented the hair; the white, the face. These dolls had no arms or legs. They were wrapped in pieces of cloth to make them look as though

Figure 34. This Blackfeet doll from the northern Plains has a wooden head and a cloth body. Tiny white beads adorn her trade-cloth dress. They represent elk's teeth and are a mark of wealth and prestige. *23/4604*

Figure 35. Tiny dolls such as these, made of scraps of leftover fabric or "pieces," were popular toys on the Plains a hundred years ago and are still made today. More elaborate than most, these two Sioux dolls wear petticoats and dresses, as well as shawls. "Pieces" dolls are not usually made in pairs, and these may represent twins. *23/8270*

they wore shawls. We had several of these shawls and used to change them like White children today change the dresses of their dolls. I had four such dolls."[10]

She also describes how children would make horses out of willow twigs and fasten the dolls to the back, pretending they were traveling. Yellow Plume maintained that Arapaho girls never played "baby" with their dolls; that they always treated the dolls like full-grown persons.

In most Plains groups, girls six or seven years old played with dolls that were quite realistic, a few of wood and the majority of cloth or buckskin. Grinnell describes how a Cheyenne girl took her doll with her everywhere, carrying it on her back in a tiny cradle-board, singing it lullabies, making clothes for it, and dressing and undressing it. This last was apparently a popular activity. Pretty Shield, a Crow medicine woman who recalled her childhood more than a hundred years ago, said she dressed and undressed her doll so often that she wore it out.[11]

Plains dolls, like their full-sized counterparts, often wore materials acquired in trade, such as beads, ribbons, and cloth. A particular favorite, one that had become a major trade item by the 1860s, was a dark blue broadcloth woven in the English woolen mills of the Stroud Valley in Gloucestershire. Known as stroud cloth or strouding, it was quickly adopted for dresses, coats, blankets, and leggings,

and scraps of stroud cloth were made into doll dresses. The Blackfeet doll in figure 34 wears such a dress, the skirt trimmed with a border of the equally popular red trade cloth.

This particular dress has another feature—a yoke decorated with dozens of the tiny white trade beads called "seed beads." The beads represent elk's teeth, a rare and precious kind of clothing decoration. Only the two upper incisor teeth were used, making the decorations extremely scarce and valuable. Like the caribou teeth belt of the Eskimo, a dress or shirt adorned with elk's teeth identified the wearer as a person of wealth and prestige. So popular are elk's teeth

house in the center of the village, where they made them dance in imitation of the ceremonial dances of their elders.

Plains

The Great Plains region of North America, extending from Saskatchewan south into Texas, is the home of numerous tribes: the Blackfeet, Crow, Sioux, Arapaho, Cheyenne, and Comanche, among others. In the nineteenth century, buffalo hunting provided food, clothing, and shelter, and warfare was a way to gain glory and honor. Accounts of Plains life at that time make clear that doll play was an integral part of childhood, remembered with pleasure by old people reminiscing about the past. Even today, in the era of commercial dolls, some are still made in the old style, and children play with both kinds.

Plains dolls are made of wood, cloth, or hide. Those made for very young children are extremely simple. A Blackfeet child's first doll might be made by her grandmother, perhaps when they go together to collect firewood. The grandmother chops a section of a birch limb about a foot long. With a knife she cuts a groove about four inches from one end to form the shoulder line, and then whittles a knoblike head with little holes to form the eyes, nose, and mouth. The limb is simply wrapped in a piece of buckskin or cloth to form the clothing.

Agnes Yellow Plume, an Arapaho woman recalling her childhood, describes another simple type of doll, known as the "pieces" doll because it is made of scraps of fabric, or "pieces." She

Figure 37. Dolls with china heads were popular on the southern Plains in the 19th century. An ancient Plains tradition appears to associate star designs with the tops of cradleboards, and on this Kiowa toy cradleboard stars are painted on the frame. *23/6804*

responsibility and the girls were given toy tipis to play with so they could learn the technique (figure 26). It was not an easy job, and two women had to work together. The long poles have to be tied together at the top at precisely the right angle, and the heavy buffalo-hide tipi cover has to be properly draped and fastened to keep out the wind and weather. Women took pride in carrying out this responsibility, and still do, although today men and boys also cooperate in putting up a tipi.

When playing together, girls arranged their toy tipis in a circle, like a grown-up camp. They lined the floor of each tipi with the skins of small animals, just as their mothers used buffalo hides. Ground-squirrel skin was a particular favorite, as the fur has a soft light-brown color mottled prettily with white. While the girls arranged their dolls and toy cradleboards, the boys played at going

Figure 38. Little Plains girls sometimes carried their dolls in toy cradleboards when moving camp. In this photograph, Pretty Beads, a Crow girl, carries her doll and cradleboard fastened to the pommel of her horse's saddle. *N41420*

hunting or making war. They might place warrior dolls on toy ponies facing in one direction and pretend that they were going on a warpath. They carried lances made of willow branches and shields made of bent willow shoots with the leafy twigs hanging down like feathers. The boys made bows and arrows of weed stalks with a prickly-pear thorn for a point. Sometimes the boys and girls divided into two enemy camps. If the girls thought the battle was going against them, they would hastily pull down the tipis, pack their possessions, and retreat. If one side captured the village, the victors would take all of the food, usually consisting of roots and grass shoots.

Another favorite "camp" game was buffalo hunting. Some children pretended to be the buffalo; others would surround and hunt them down, riding sticks for horses and lashing them with their quirts to make them run fast. If a real buffalo hunt were going on at the same time, a good-natured hunter might give the children some pieces of real buffalo meat to use in playing camp. Pretty Shield recalled a time when a group of girls had set up play camp nicely, with tipis and dolls, and decided that they needed to get a real buffalo to make things right. They managed, after much effort, to kill a buffalo calf, but it was such a struggle getting it back that "it looked pretty bad by the time we got it to our play-village."[14]

Children still "play camp" today. It is a valuable exercise in learning role models and necessary skills—and it is fun, undoubtedly the reason for its continuing popularity.

Eastern North America

The people of northeastern North America, who grow "the three sisters"—corn, beans, and squash—use the cornhusks gathered at the harvest for a variety of purposes, among them making dolls. Cornhusk dolls are actually made in many parts of the Americas but the dolls of the Iroquois people are the best known. Some sources state that cornhusk dolls were initially used only in medicine rites, but by the nineteenth century cornhusk dolls made as children's toys were on the scene.

The early English settlers in the east also made cornhusk dolls for their children. They probably learned the art from the Indians, for although harvest figures made of sheaves of wheat were common throughout Europe corn was not as well known there. Arthur

Parker, a Seneca historian who has written about the cornhusk dolls of the Northeast, stated that they were dressed both as men and women and furnished with miniature bows and arrows or cooking pots.

Iroquois cornhusk dolls used in medicine ceremonies were always made without faces, but by the nineteenth century dolls for play were sometimes faceless and sometimes not. One explanation was that "no-face" dolls allowed a child to develop imagination. Some Iroquois people offered another reason for "no-face" dolls: if a child played too roughly or injured her doll in some way, it would not be able to identify the culprit and bring a punishment.[15] The implication that a doll might have such power suggests an association with its use in medicine ceremonies.

Figure 39. In the 19th century, some of the Mahican people moved from their homes in the Northeast to the Stockbridge settlement in Wisconsin. They continued to make traditional cornhusk dolls. This one, dressed in plaid cotton trade cloth, has an unusually large head and hair made of buffalo hair. *16/5487*

A Seneca story of the Doll-with-no-face offers yet another explanation. The story tells of a cornhusk doll whose face was so lovely that she became extremely vain. Finally one day, the Great Spirit removed her beautiful features. She had to undertake a long and dangerous journey through a woods filled with frightening monsters in order to reach the spirit who would restore her looks. As she traveled along the way, several spirit helpers assisted her, and she learned courage, humility, and the virtues of contentment. The story of the Doll-with-no-face, a favorite among Seneca children, serves to reinforce moral values.

In addition to cornhusk dolls, the Seneca and Oneida people also make apple-head dolls for children. The head is begun by peeling and coring a green apple, gently molding the features to shape, and hanging it up to dry. Each day the features are molded further until the apple finally looks like a small human face. Such apple heads, attached to a cornhusk body, represent a being called Loose-Feet, who grants wishes to little children.

Ojibwe children of Wisconsin and Minnesota have several kinds of dolls. One type is the "dancing doll," made of a bunch of Norway pine needles tied together and cut square on the bottom like a broom. It can be set upright on a tin pan and, as a child gently shakes the pan, it dances. Other Ojibwe dolls are made of green basswood leaves or bright-colored autumn leaves fastened together with little splinters of wood. Ojibwe children also play with small figures of dried bull rush root tied with basswood fiber, and with dolls made of willow twigs dressed in scraps of cloth. The figures represent both men and women, as do "paper" dolls cut from the inner bark of the slippery elm tree. Such dolls are cut in simple shapes, easily held by little hands, and usually do not last very long.

When cloth and beads became available, mothers began making cloth dolls stuffed with moss and with embroidered or painted faces. Girls often received their first lessons in sewing and bead-work by helping to dress their dolls and decorate toy cradleboards. Ojibwe cradleboards have a characteristic feature that the toy cradleboard in figure 40 reflects faithfully—the addition of a small hoop filled with webbing dangling from the frame. It represents a spider web and is intended to protect the baby from any ill fortune that might approach, catching it just as a spider catches a fly in its web.

Dolls and their accoutrements are decorated not only with bead-work but also with ribbonwork. This is a technique of cutting ribbon into patterns and appliquéing it as a decorative edging on blankets, leggings, moccasins, and other clothing. Ribbonwork, a uniquely Native American art form, was developed by Indian women when French fur traders began bringing ribbons to North America early in the eighteenth century. After the French Revolution in the 1780s, court dress fell into disrepute and vast quantities of ribbon from the French silk factories of Tours and Lyon became a glut on the market. Fur trading companies shipped the excess ribbon to North America, where Indian women accepted it with delight. Ribbonwork as a decorative art form is still popular today, and tribally distinct styles decorate dresses, shirts, and dance leggings.

Figure 40. The toy cradleboard for this doll is adorned with Ojibwe floral beadwork on black velvet panels. Although little girls often decorated toy cradleboards, this particular one was probably fashioned by an adult, for the velvet strips are taken from a man's shirt or leggings and have been reused. *12/2180*

Figure 41. This Cree doll of Canada depicts an old woman wearing a long belted tunic and knee-high leggings in traditional style. Her carefully braided long white hair is fastened with strips of red ribbon. A trade blanket of English wool keeps out the cold. *24/1833*

Cree children of eastern Canada dress their dolls in clothing designed for warmth. Cree women traditionally wore long belted tunics and warm leggings. They wrapped themselves in rabbit skin blankets, or woolen trade blankets when those became available. The doll in figure 41 is dressed in this nineteenth-century style. Most Cree dolls are carved from wood, and they are often outfitted with miniature snowshoes and birchbark canoes.

While dolls have been reported and described throughout the Northeast, there is little recorded information about toy dolls among the Indian children of the southeastern United States. Foreign settlers overran this area at a very early period. The Cherokee, Choctaw, Chickasaw, Creek, and the Seminole, some of whom were descendants of the great Mississippian chiefdoms (see *From the Past*), were caught in the struggle for power among the English, the Spanish, and the French. One of the blackest chapters in American history is the forcible removal in the 1830s of many of the Southeast peoples to Oklahoma on the journey known as The Trail of Tears. Those who stayed—the Seminole in the Florida Everglades, some Cherokee in the mountains of North Carolina, a number of Choctaw in Mississippi, and others—today make dolls for sale to outsiders (see *For Purchase*). One account from the turn of the century stated that Seminole children played with a simple type of doll described as "a stick with a lot of cloth wrapped around it." Seminole children built houses, called "camps," for their dolls. They were probably copies of the *chickee*, the thatch-roofed, open-sided houses still in use today, cleverly designed to provide shade and allow for tropical breezes to cool the occupants.

The Southwest

The southwestern United States is a land of mountains and deserts, cliffs and canyons, sagebrush and cactus. The people who live here, some of whom settled thousands of years ago, have adapted to the dry climate in various ways. In the 1800s, most Apache people existed by hunting, gathering, and raiding. The Navajo began raising sheep when the Spanish arrived in the sixteenth century and still do so today. The Pueblo people are desert farmers, cultivating corn and beans through careful management of the scarce water.

Morris Opler, an anthropologist who worked for many years with the Apache people, learned how girls are taught adult skills and described what happens as follows: "The mother lets the little girl help sew the doll's dress the first time. The next time she teaches her how to sew and tells her to do it herself. The mother teaches her how to cook for the dolls, too . . . and she tells her how to feed the dolls, for someday the girl is going to be a mother and have children."[16]

Apache dolls were made of a forked stick with horsehair attached to the "head" end to simulate human hair. This rudimentary head is often elegantly adorned with earrings. Necklaces and other jewelry are often added, too. Doll clothes also replicate traditional Apache dresses, which are elaborately decorated with fringe, paint, cloth appliqué, and tiny metal danglers that make a jingling sound with every movement (figure 42).

The Navajo are among the few Native American peoples who did not traditionally make dolls as children's toys, for representations of the human form are used only in a few religious contexts. This sensitivity was somewhat relaxed in the twentieth century. In the 1940s, children made and played with dolls fashioned from pine needles and sugar sacks (figure 2). Doll making was a craft project at the Ramah Day School on the Navajo reservation,[17] and the Indian Arts and Crafts Board acquired a number of dolls from doll makers in the 1960s (see *For Purchase*). Children today also play with store-bought dolls. Even today, however, the more conservative people frown on dolls. R. W. Lang reports that a crew of Navajo workmen refused to continue working at an archaeological site when some wooden figurines were unearthed there. And when children do play with dolls, there is a strong feeling that a doll should not be mistreated or broken, although, as one Navajo man said, "If you handle it nicely, it probably won't hurt you."[18] A worn-out or broken doll is not thrown away but left carefully in a secluded place so that it will not bring illness to anyone.

Figure 42. This Chiricahua Apache doll wears a classic two-piece woman's hide dress. Both top and skirt are heavily fringed and dyed with yellow ocher; a band of cloth appliqué and a row of metal danglers decorate them. The dress is also adorned with brass upholstery tacks and paper fasteners, which give the effect of metal studs. The metal cones may have been cut from tin cans. *16/1347*

This scarcity of dolls among the Navajo contrasts sharply with the abundance of dolls made by their nearby neighbors, the Hopi. From the Pueblo villages of the Southwest comes one of the most colorful and complex of all Native American doll forms—the katsina doll, or *tihu* (*tithu* in the plural). Tithu are carved and painted images of katsinas, powerful supernatural beings who personify the spirit essence of everything in the real world—ancestor spirits, natural forces, and plant and animal life forms.

Katsinas and tithu are best understood as part of a rich ceremonial complex found throughout the Pueblos, especially in the western regions among the Zuni and the Hopi. For over 1,000 years, Pueblo people have lived in adobe villages scattered from the Rio Grande Valley in New Mexico, to the dry, high mesa country of northern Arizona. These desert farmers grow corn, beans, and squash in a difficult, arid land. The balance of nature is precarious, and the threat of drought, flash floods, hailstorms, and other natural disasters hangs heavy over the growing season.

The focus of ceremonial life is an annual cycle of rituals centering on the need for rain, fertility, and general well-being. For the Hopi, the period from the winter solstice in mid-December to the first harvest in July is the time when the katsinas descend from their home in the San Francisco Mountains to appear in the villages as masked dancers (see *For Performance*). Their arrival coincides with preparations for the planting season, and their dances and ritual observances are intended to bring rain and good weather to nurture the crops. Katsinas bring many blessings: good weather,

Figure 43. Hopi girls receive katsina dolls as gifts during certain ceremonies. Emry Kopta took this photograph of a little Hopi girl in the 1930s. Courtesy Museum of Northern Arizona.

fertility, happiness, and long life. During the time they remain in the villages, they initiate young children into the katsina societies, and reinforce good behavior and the social values of cooperation and hard work that are an important part of Pueblo life.

Tithu traditionally are given as gifts during certain ceremonies. At the end of the Powamuy Ceremony that initiates the growing season, the katsina dancers present tithu as gifts to all the little girls, with a prayer-wish that they may grow up healthy and strong, and be blessed with many children. Children play with their tithu just as they play with other dolls, carrying them around as all children do.

The simple, flat doll known as *putsqatihu* is often the first toy given to infant girls, and in some villages to baby boys. Said to represent Hahay'iwuuti, the mother of all the katsinas, it has a body painted with vertical red lines and arms and shoulders painted alternately in green and yellow. The colors, as on all tithu, symbolize the six directions—north, south, east, west, up, and down. The putsqatihu can be tied to a full-size cradleboard or given its own miniature one, to be played with as a doll and cradle set. They are also given to brides, and in some pueblos, to a woman who wishes to have a child.

Much of the Western literature on tithu states that their primary purpose is as a learning device, to help children recognize the many different types of katsinas. No doubt they do serve this function, but the gift of a tihu to a little Hopi girl means, for her and her family, a blessing, happiness, and spiritual connections with Hopi people from the past and future.

Central and South America

Ranging from the Rio Grande River to the tip of Tierra del Fuego, Central and South America are regions of great geographical and cultural diversity. Rocky deserts, lush tropical jungles, high mountains, and low-lying swamplands set the scene for a variety of peoples, from remote hunters and gatherers to residents of great cities. Many areas of Central and South America have been occupied by the Spanish for more than 400 years, and the people living there show a cultural blend of Native lifeways intertwined with elements of Spanish Catholicism. In other places, far from the paths of commerce and conquest, the occasional traveler receives the impression that life has persisted unchanged for centuries. The impression is

false, for European influence has encroached on virtually all the Native peoples of the Western Hemisphere in one form or another. Nevertheless, traditional ways continue. In agricultural areas, farmers still grow corn in fields cleared by burning. Women still weave cloth with a backstrap loom. Children continue to play with dolls that reflect their cultural heritage.

Two wooden dolls from Mexico are illustrated in figures 44 and 45. Carved from soft wood and decorated with splashes of bright paint, they typify the homemade playthings reported from villages throughout Mexico and Central America. Some dolls are purchased in village markets—for example, wooden puppets and the papier-mâché jointed dolls to be discussed later (see *For Purchase*). Doll play imitates such adult activities as cooking, childcare, and preparing

Figure 44. Children in northern Mexico treasure these small dolls, made by their fathers from scraps of wood and dressed in fragments of cloth. The movable arms are attached by straight pins. *22/8740*

Figure 45. The shape of this brightly painted Zapotec wooden doll from Oaxaca, Mexico, strongly resembles stone figures found in nearby archaeological sites. *21/8807*

for and participating in fiestas. The little doll from northern Mexico carries on her back a scrap of wood that is almost certainly intended to represent a baby. Her stick-like arms are fastened to the body with straight pins, and she wears a hair ornament of tiny beads, evidence that even the simplest of dolls are fashioned with some care.

The rough, somewhat chunky shape of the Zapotec doll from Oaxaca is strongly reminiscent of the small carved stone figures found in nearby archaeological sites. Whether it represents a continuation of an ancient carving style is not known; its form may well have been inspired by that of the earlier figures, collected by the local people today and sometimes placed in shrines or used as household decorations.

The Seri people of the Sonoran Desert, in northwestern Mexico, are reported to make several kinds of dolls. Older women used to make toys for children modeled after the clay figures found in local archaeological sites. Seri children also play with tiny dolls fashioned of scraps of cloth, made without features and often without arms (figure 46). They range in size from five or six inches to less than an inch high. This kind of doll is not only a toy but is nowadays sold to tourists. In the past, it was also used as a fetish or grave offering. An account published in 1898 states that women were buried with domestic implements and with one or more small dolls, made either entirely of cloth or of a piece of deer bone dressed in a cloth skirt fastened with string.[19]

Like their owners, dolls from the highlands of Guatemala wear clothing woven at home that conforms strictly to the style of each village. Embroidered designs often decorate the fabric; one of the popular motifs, a row of stylized human figures, is called *muñecas*, or "dolls." Most dolls are carved of wood, either in one solid piece or with movable limbs, but occasionally a commercially made china doll is acquired and dressed in the same fashion.

The Guatemalan doll in figure 47 wears a *tzut*, or scarf, on the head. Tzuts are squares of cloth, of various sizes and fabrics, used by both men and women for everything from carrying babies to covering food. Men frequently wear a tzut as a head covering and top it with a hat of palm leaf or straw. This doll may originally have worn such a hat. It also wears a sash, an item of clothing worn in Central America since before the time of the Spanish. Each village not only has its own style of weaving sashes but also of tying them. Even in areas where clothing has become thoroughly modernized, the sash remains an article of traditional wear.

Toy dolls also are reported throughout the South American continent. Along the Orinoco River, little girls play with wooden dolls made by their fathers; among the Cashinahua of eastern Peru it is the mothers who make their children clay dolls with clamshell eyes and with sexual features clearly marked. South American dolls, like their northern counterparts, are equipped with various kinds of accessories such as doll-sized manos and metates for grinding corn. Warrau fathers of Venezuela make doll hammocks for their little girls, and Cashinahua children, among others, use small clay cooking pots and water jars to add authenticity to their play.

Designs of tattooing or body paint, widely used throughout the tropics to add beauty to the human form, often decorate dolls from tropical areas as well. The Shipibo-Conibo of the Amazon lowlands,

Figure 47. This Quiche man is dressed in hand-woven cotton from highland Guatemala. His trousers, with rows of embroidered designs, may illustrate those worn for a special occasion such as the fiesta held on a saint's name day. Everyday trousers from this area are of plain white cotton. *22/4791*

Figure 48. Karaja children of Brazil play with their dolls as a way of imitating the grownup activities around them. These three dolls include a woman holding a large bowl, meant to hold manioc cakes; a mother holding her child; and a young girl playing with either a doll or a baby. Dolls like this, decorated with accurate renderings of Karaja body paint, are made today not only as toys but also for sale in the tourist market. *23/1562*

for example, have an ancient tradition of covering not only their own bodies but houses, boats, paddles, textiles, and pottery with delicate geometric painting in interlocking lines. "Everything is covered with designs," says a Shipibo-Conibo song. For these people, the material and the spiritual worlds are overlain with fine lines in symbolic patterns that express cosmic significance. The Great World Boa whose body encircles the universe; the "eye-soul," symbol of human life; and the stylized cross, possibly derived from the shape of the human figure, all appear as motifs in painted body decoration and on household objects. The balsa toy dolls of the Shipibo-Conibo, which show the same designs, are carved by men and painted by the women, who are considered the artists. Many dolls are also dressed in skirts and shawls or ponchos like those the people wear. Similar painted dolls are made by neighboring peoples such as the Yagua, who use them as grave markers. But the Shipibo-Conibo not only make them as children's toys but today produce them to sell in the burgeoning tourist market.

The Karaja people of the Brazilian rain forest make dolls of clay that also wear body paint, reflecting the real world (figure 48). Like the Shipibo-Conibo dolls, these are traditional toys now made also to sell to tourists. A favorite game among Karaja children is to imitate with their dolls the intricate movements of the traditional *aruaña* dance. The aruaña is a fish, a mainstay of life, and the sinuous fishlike movements of the dancers are intended to ensure its return each year. An aruaña dance has four participants. Two men wear elaborate costumes of straw and tropical bird feathers with designs representing the fish. Two women dance side by side facing the men. As they sing the appropriate songs and move together along a dance track at the edge of the village, the children watch and listen. During their play, the children set up a dance track in the sand next to the river, sing the songs, and imitate the prescribed dance movements with their dolls. Thus they learn the songs and dances they will need to know when they grow up.

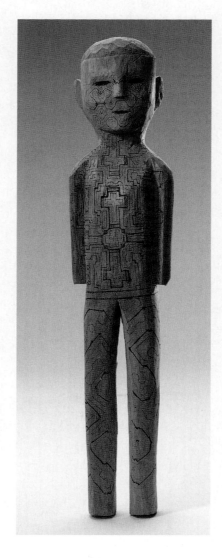

Figure 49. Balsa dolls among the Shipibo-Conibo of eastern Peru are called Mosho Joni, or "balsa person." The painted body designs have persisted despite 300 years of missionary activity, although the meaning of some of them has been lost. *23/1613*

The Karaja dolls are quite realistic, but other South American toy dolls have a more abstract appearance. In the Gran Chaco region of Paraguay, for example, favorite toys of Lengua children are tiny dolls made from animal knucklebones. Lengua mothers also make clay dolls for their children, highly conventionalized female forms described as "a conical clump of clay with two breasts." Despite their rudimentary design, the facial tattooing and hair are carefully indicated with engraved lines.

Tapirapé toy dolls from Brazil are made of black beeswax with sticks for arms and legs (figure 50). Beeswax dolls from the same area made for ritual purposes are more likely to be adorned with feathers, shells, and down (figure 65 in *For Power*). Play dolls and

Figure 50. Indians of the Amazon rain forest use beeswax to make dolls of all sizes. Some, elaborately decorated with featherwork, are made for ritualistic purposes, but plain dolls such as this Tapirapé one are toys. *23/1510*

Figure 51. Sturdy dolls made for very young children are carved from a single block of wood with no parts to break off. This one from Ecuador is probably a type made for a ceremony of dedication for the child, after which it became a plaything. *2/3594*

ritual dolls clearly differ, despite the basic similarities in materials and form.

Throughout the northwestern part of South America and into Panama, there exist dolls of another kind, in which the sacred and secular are combined. These carved wooden dolls of simple form are often made with a base so that they can stand. Their sturdiness and lack of sharp edges make them ideal toys for very young children and, indeed, they are used in this way. Each one, however, is made by a shaman and begins its existence as a sacred object, intended to contain the guardian spirit of an infant. During a ceremony of dedication, the spirit passes from the figure into the child, after which the doll is given to the child for a plaything. The wooden doll from Ecuador illustrated in figure 51, described as "made for very young children," is almost certainly one of these figures. The Caduveo in Brazil may have similar dolls. One report

states that, while children played with them, they were also identified with Christian saints. It may be that the concept of a doll as an object both sacred and secular exists in a fairly wide area.

Dolls made of or dressed in various kinds of cloth are not rare, but dolls knitted out of yarn seem to be confined, in the historic period, to the Andean region of Bolivia and Peru, where the Quechua people live in the mountain valleys, and the Aymara occupy the highlands. The Aymara are described as a "textile-minded" people, for whom spinning and weaving are major occupations. Men, women, and children are seen spinning thread with a spindle whorl and shaft as they walk the paths of the Bolivian Andes or gossip in the marketplace. Spinning metaphors appear in other areas of life; the Aymara way of getting rid of bad spirits is to go through the motions of spinning in reverse.

Figure 52. Quechua male and female knitted dolls from the Andes are traditionally made for children, but these, fashioned of fine yarn and finished with silk floss and sequins, were designed to sell. The man carries a baby llama, the woman a spindle filled with thread. *10/7592* [man], *10/7593* [woman]

Figure 53. Knitted into the skirt of this Quechua woman are tiny designs of animals, designs found in ancient Peruvian weavings as well as in contemporary clothing. *23/9922*

Women of the region are said to be "surpassingly clever" at knitting, producing compartmented moneybags and containers for coca leaves in the shape of animals or people. The dolls the Aymara and the Quechua make for their children reflect this great skill, having knitted heads and bodies dressed in jackets and trousers or long-skirted dresses with small designs knitted into the fabric (figures 52 and 53). All kinds of fibers are knitted into dolls, but the most common material is llama wool, with silk being used in recent years to make dolls for sale. Many dolls carry spindle whorls, reflecting the importance of spinning as a daily activity.

Dolls for play seem to exist almost everywhere throughout the Americas, although the information for some areas is quite full and for others very scanty. Not every observer considered children's activities worthy of mention. There are enough examples, however, to indicate that dolls are an important part of childhood and to suggest that doll play provides both an educational and an emotional component. Dolls are educational in that children playing with them learn both practical techniques and attitudes of adult behavior. Dolls are also emotionally satisfying not only for the child who learns love and caring but also for the parent who take pleasure in making a toy that will bring delight.

FOR POWER

DOLLS HAVE SERVED IN MANY human quests: as a means to heal or harm; to bring good weather, fertile crops, or abundant game; to foretell the future; to bring the blessing of children or the curse of madness or death; to entice a lover or to assure the well-being of the world; to summon supernatural forces; to bring good fortune; or to exorcise evil spirits. Often, these uses for dolls have related to two ancient religious and spiritual concepts: animism and shamanism. Both are found throughout the world in traditional societies, not only among hunters and gatherers but also farmers and herders. Animism is the belief that not only human beings but also animals, physical objects, and natural forces are imbued with spirits. People can reach and influence these spirits through prayers, self-purification, and dreams, and they often create doll figures to personify animistic power.

The concept of shamanism revolves around those few individuals who become religious specialists, especially gifted in what Eliade called "the technique of ecstasy."[1] They can transcend their physical being and communicate with supernatural forces, acting as intermediaries between the worlds of the known and the unknown. Such men and women are often called shamans. Technically, the term "shaman" applies only to such individuals among the Tungus of Siberia, but many religious specialists elsewhere have similar abilities. The Eskimo *angakok*, the Tlingit *ix't*, the Huichol *mara'akame*, and other gifted men and women from virtually every

Figure 54. This Quechua doll represents Ekeko, the traditional god of good fortune in the Andean highlands. He is bedecked with miniature objects, each standing for a specific wish: cloth sacks containing rice, sugar, and candy cigarettes; a wooden truck and a wicker airplane; a large knife; and assorted household furnishings. *21/8519*

group in the Americas are able to cure illness, foretell the future, bring good or evil fortune, and influence the weather and the movements of game animals. In the special equipment they use, shamans often include doll figures along with drums and rattles, masks, and bone tubes for sucking illness from patients.

The concepts of animism and shamanism go far back in human history. The cave paintings and "Venus" figurines of the Upper Paleolithic period in Europe and Asia may be early expressions of such beliefs. Perhaps they were part of the cultural baggage inherited from the first hunting peoples thousands of years ago.

As certain dolls are made and used only by shamans or other specialists, others are created by ordinary individuals in response to a wish, a vision, or a dream. Some are displayed openly, such as the small ivory figures fastened to the deck of an Eskimo kayak to assure hunting success. Others are carefully hidden away in sacred medicine bundles and revealed only within the context of a special ceremony and to certain individuals. Some dolls are handed down from one generation to the next as repositories of spiritual power. Others are made for a particular ritual and discarded when they have served their purpose.

One of the most widespread functions of dolls as expressions of spiritual power is in their use as fertility figures. An Eskimo woman who wanted a baby would be directed by the shaman to sleep with a small ivory doll under her pillow. Certain Plains medicine bundles held miniature dolls in cradleboards used to help barren women. In the pueblos of the Southwest during the spring Bean Dance Ceremony, women throw cornmeal toward masked dancers carrying dolls, a petition to have a child. A particular kind of flat katsina doll called a *putsqatihu* and representing "the mother of the katsinas" is given not only to Hopi brides but also to women who have suffered a miscarriage. In Oaxaca, Mexico, childless couples make a pilgrimage to a sacred place such as a cave or an altar in the mountains. Here they make a miniature doll and cradle, and as the woman holds the doll to her breast and rocks it, they implore the spirits for a child.

People of the Eastern Woodlands and the Great Lakes use dolls for a variety of religious and ceremonial purposes. During the rites of the Midewiwin, or Medicine Lodge Society, members display and manipulate effigies of the guardian spirits they have received in a dream, evidence of the owner's supernatural powers. Other individuals

Figure 55. Mountain Chief, Piegan Blackfeet veteran of the 19th-century intertribal wars on the northern Plains, holds a miniature horse and rider. These effigies commemorated war exploits such as the taking of a horse from the enemy and were used in reenactments of the victories. Such ceremonies and the use of similar effigies were performed as part of Blackfeet victory dances as late as 1910. Courtesy of the Smithsonian Institution National Anthropological Archives. Photograph by Joseph Dixon Wanamaker Expedition, date not recorded. ©April 30, 1913. Negative #75-11151.

make small figures appear to come alive and dance, as a demonstration of their abilities to control psychic forces. Midé doctors, diviners, and curers had different kinds of abilities, but eighteenth-century French and English observers lumped them all together as "Jugglers": individuals who dazzled and confused the uninitiated by the performance of some feats that have never been explained such as moving unseen from one tent to another within the view of skeptical witnesses. An observer in 1710 described how the Jugglers would "show the amazing effects of their knowledge and powers"[2] by performing tricks, among them animation of Juggler dolls. The use of the dolls seems to have served two purposes: as a public demonstration of personal power within the Midewiwin as well as separate from it, and for personal medicine and divination.

Midé doctors used carved wooden dolls to cure the sick, but they could also use those same dolls to bring evil. An early nineteenth-century traveler to North America reported on an Ojibwe Midewiwin practitioner who could cause pain to an enemy by running needles into the head or heart of a wooden doll.[3] By burning or burying such a figure he even had the power to kill.

Using dolls to perform ceremonies invoking harm is a practice that exists worldwide. It is probably an extension of the ancient belief in animism and the possibility of influencing events and persons by the manipulation of objects. The witch turning a small

Figure 56. This doll represents a wealthy Potawatomi woman who is probably a priestess of the Midewiwin society. Her powers are seen in the "bear-claw" pendant, the beaded charm bag of the kind used for sacred medicine, and the leather paint bag probably containing vermilion, a pigment used in curing. The stick in her belt is possibly a prescription stick that would be marked with formulas for administering herbal medicines. *24/1799*

Figure 57. This photograph was taken at a Doll Dance in Oklahoma some time before 1947. The women are pounding corn to be made into cakes and eaten at the feast following the ceremony. Inside the tent three dolls are visible attached to the poles. Photograph possibly by Lula Mae Gibson Galliland. Courtesy of the Smithsonian Institution National Anthropological Archives. Negative #55, 658.

effigy of the victim over a fire; the sorcerer running thorns through the head of a clay figure to kill an enemy; the supplicant burning a doll of twigs with hair from an intended victim—all share the same awareness that miniature renderings of human beings can have a presence and a power larger than themselves.

Just as some dolls serve in the summoning of dark and unknown forces, so others are beneficent figures, guardians of good health and bringers of blessings and various kinds of luck. Among the most powerful of these is the Health Guardian doll made by the Delaware people and referred to as "Our Grandmother." The Unami Delaware refer to their Health Guardian figure as "Odas," while the Minsi Delaware call theirs "Nanitis." Such dolls belong to particular families and are treated with the greatest respect and veneration. An Unami story of the origin of the Odas figure was told to M. R. Harrington in the early 1900s as follows:

Long ago some children, playing with sticks, decided to cut faces upon them, and were then very much surprised to notice that the little dolls that they had thus made seemed to have life. Their parents made them throw the dolls away when they discovered this, and most of the children soon forgot what had happened. One little girl, however, grieved for her doll; it bothered her all the time and finally she began to dream of it every night. Then she told her parents of her trouble, and they realized that they should not have compelled her to throw the doll away. One night the doll appeared to the child and spoke to her, saying, "Find me and keep me always, and you and your family will ever enjoy good health. You must give me clothing and hold a dance for me every spring," and told her exactly what to do. The girl reported this to her parents, who immediately looked for the doll and found it, then dressed it, made some hominy, killed a deer, and held a dance in its honor as they were instructed, and this rite has been continued to the present day.[4]

The first Nanitis among the Minsi Delaware was said to have been made on the advice of a shaman, to cure a man seriously ill. One man reported that his mother had had such a doll, and that every year she made three sets of new clothing for it, including new moccasins. It seemed to her that her doll "sometimes went about of its own accord, although she kept it carefully in a box, for the old dresses always seemed worn at the bottom and soiled, and she found burrs clinging to them when she went to put new clothes on. . . ."[5]

A report written by a missionary in 1839 describes a Health Guardian doll, said to be more than 100 years old, "fantastically arrayed in Indian costume and nearly covered with silver brooches and trinkets; . . . and was kept wrapped up in some 20 envelopments of broad-cloth trimmed with scarlet ribbon."[6]

Among the Delaware, the annual feast in honor of the Health Guardian doll is sponsored by one or more families who own one. Dressed in a new outfit and adorned with necklaces of beads or shell, the doll is fastened to a dance pole and addressed by a speaker, who asks it to bring good health to the family of its owner. As he dances and sings, people fall in line behind him, men in one line and women in another. At the end of each dance the pole is passed to the next person until twelve dances have been performed, matching the number of the twelve heavens and the twelve moons. The dance ends with a feast of hominy and venison, a joyous occasion marking the assurance that good health and good fortune will prevail during the coming year.

An interesting variation of the tradition of Health Guardian dolls is shown in figure 58, which illustrates two cloth dolls collected by M. R. Harrington in 1909 from the Shawnee of Oklahoma. Harrington's field notes describe these as Ni-tcap-ka-win, or "effigies of the dead," and state that once a year a feast was made at which the dolls took the place of the deceased and were honored as if they were the actual persons.[7] The dolls expressed a continuing relationship with those who had "passed over" and the recognition that the deceased still had an important role in the well-being of the family.

Not all dolls representing the deceased were as realistic as those of the Shawnee. Ojibwe mothers in the Lake Superior area who had lost a child sometimes made a "doll of misfortune," composed of feathers. The woman would carry the doll on her back, along with her child's clothes and toys, and she cared for the doll as if caring

Figure 58. Two of a group collected from the Shawnee of Oklahoma, these dolls are described as portraits of persons who have died and who are remembered at a memorial feast in their honor. The similarities in workmanship such as the use of beads for the facial features suggest that the same person made them. They are dressed in the mid-to-late 19th-century style of clothing worn by the Shawnee. The man wears a ruffled "hunting coat" copied from a European garment and carries a beaded shoulder bag, traditional features of men's clothing throughout eastern North America. The woman's calico blouse is decorated with a metal brooch. Both dolls wear cloth leggings carefully trimmed with ribbonwork. *2/1863* [woman], *2/1871* [man]

for her child in the next world, until the child would be old enough to take care of herself or himself. Among the Sioux, grief-stricken parents would sometimes keep an effigy of their child in the form of a carved pole dressed in clothing.[8] While they kept the "ghost pole," usually for up to a year, the family observed strict rules of mourning behavior and curtailed many activities. Keeping a ghost pole was a heavy responsibility, but it assuaged sorrow and helped keep the child's presence close.

Dolls such as the Delaware Health Guardian figures, which belong to a deep and profound religious complex, were never made for outsiders. But another kind of "good fortune" doll, the Aymara Ekeko figure of Bolivia, which incorporates elements of Catholic ritual, has also become a popular item to sell to tourists (figures 54 and 59).

Ekeko is a jolly, smiling dwarf, sometimes referred to as a "peddler doll" because he is burdened with so many miniature objects that he seems almost to disappear under the load—boxes, sacks, baskets and jars, small cars or airplanes, and miniature candies or cigarettes. Ekeko may be of pre-Columbian origin. An observer from early Spanish colonial times stated that "Ecaco" was the same deity as Tunupa, a major sky-god related to the Andean supreme being, Viracocha. It is certainly true that miniature objects of various kinds have been found in Andean archaeological sites and may have been made for similar figures.

Ekeko dolls are kept on Aymara household altars, and each of the miniature objects bedecking them represents a wish for a specific kind of good fortune. Each year a great fair is held in January, the fiesta of *alacitas*. Its name comes from the cry of the merchants, "Buy (from me)!" The markets are filled with hundreds of stalls selling miniatures of all kinds that are made to adorn Ekeko. Each purchaser carefully chooses objects symbolizing wishes for the coming year. In La Paz, as the cathedral bells ring at the stroke of noon, everyone flocks into the church to have the miniatures blessed by the priest, a remarkable blending of traditions.

Like the Aymara people, many non-Indians believe fervently in the power of Ekeko to grant wishes, and they also purchase their miniatures with care and lavishly adorn the little figures. In recent years a New York mail order house has sold Ekeko figures as "good

Figure 59. Ekeko, believed to have the power to grant wishes, presides over many Aymara household altars in Bolivia. *21/8519*

luck" dolls, and the blessings Ekeko brings have spread far from his original Andean home.

Some dolls can bring blessings; others are used as oracles to see into the future and predict success in ventures such as hunting. The Yukon Eskimo had a yearly festival that centered on a wooden doll; after the ceremony the doll was wrapped in birchbark and hidden in a tree. From time to time, the doll was fed with fish or caribou meat, and it was said that if the year promised to be a good one for hunting or fishing, the shaman would find caribou hair or fish scales in the wrappings.

Another type of wooden doll showing oracular powers and usable in hunting magic was the Tree Dweller figure of the eastern forests of North America. The Tree Dweller, an elf-like supernatural creature of frightening demeanor, was believed to live deep in the woods in the stump of a hollow tree. His power took the form of an enchanted cylindrical shaft extending upward into the sky. Birds flying over the shaft were stricken dead and fell into the Tree Dweller's den, where they were eaten. Even the powerful thunderbird was reported to avoid his home. The Tree Dweller was apt to seek out a lonely hunter in the woods and fire at him a volley of confusing questions. If the hunter answered any question with a "yes," the first person in his family whom he met thereafter would die, for the Tree Dweller's question was always a request for a human life.

Nevertheless, Tree Dwellers were venerated for their power to guarantee hunting success and to foretell the future. One account states that a Tree Dweller doll once predicted to its owner a successful raid against the Ojibwe, saying that the warrior who carried the medicine bundle containing the doll would strike the first blow on the enemy. All happened as foretold, and the doll was awarded an eagle feather.[9]

Tree Dweller dolls were kept in a boxlike "hollow tree," carved of wood and sometimes decorated with images of supernatural beings. One report states that the "tree" was made from a cottonwood trunk cut down by two young men "who had never yet spoken to a woman."[10] The right to make and use a Tree Dweller doll was granted when an individual saw one in a dream or vision. "Tree Dweller dreamers" were described as a special cult among the Teton Lakota, and members of the group employed their powers to cure illness. Members of the Medicine Dance Society of the Wahpeton

Lakota used an image of the Tree Dweller as one of their patrons, and owners of a Tree Dweller doll were reported to be successful hunters. Information about precisely how the doll was used is sparse, but one description exists of a curing ceremony carried out by a Yanktonai Lakota shaman in North Dakota.[11] He placed the doll in a box filled with pulverized wood, covered it with a red cloth, and caused the doll to dance in time to drumming. This animation of the doll, so like the Midewiwin figures and Juggler dolls of the East, may represent a western dimension of that widespread tradition.

People throughout the Americas also use dolls in the performance of love medicine. Often the dolls are made as male/female pairs. Love medicine is sometimes viewed with mixed feelings; to the Ojibwe, it is akin to sorcery and the stealing of another person's soul, to be attempted only when everything else has failed. A report of Ojibwe love magic dating from 1825 describes the procedure as pricking the heart of the image of the beloved and inserting a magic powder into the puncture,[12] all the while beseeching that the love will be returned. Another method is placing the dolls face to face, together with some hair from the loved one, and tying them tightly together with cords while performing a series of incantations. Pulling the cords is intended to make the beloved feel a pull of attraction from which there is no escape. The wooden medicine dolls of the Great Lakes area were painted with mercury vermilion before each use, perhaps because red is widely considered the color of life.

Among the people of the Plains, dolls were included in love medicine bundles. Men or women who had suffered the grief of unrequited love and had received a vision owned them. A lovelorn petitioner would ask for help from the owner of such a bundle. One account of a powerful Crow medicine man states that when he was approached by a woman asking for help, he would face her in the direction of the man's tipi, place the male doll at the back of her head, and perform the appropriate rituals and songs to help her win the man's love. He would perform the same ritual for a man, but this time would use the female doll.[13]

While some love medicine dolls are intimately connected with dreams or visions, others have more mundane origins. In the markets of La Paz, Bolivia, Aymara people can buy small male and female figures intended to offer help in love affairs. Made of marl, a kind of clay, they are placed face to face, wrapped in wool, blessed with a sacrificial offering, and left on an altar on the mountainside. Alternatively, they may be left at the loved one's door, or placed in his/her clothing. They are said to have an aphrodisiac effect.

Of all the religious ceremonies practiced by the Native people of the Americas, one of the best known may be the Sun Dance, the sacred ceremony performed by some twenty Plains groups. Held in the summer, it is sponsored by an individual who has made a personal vow to do so. Only two Plains peoples, the Kiowa and the Crow, use a doll as a central feature, but in each case the Sun Dance doll is a supremely sacred and powerful figure.

Many Plains groups make the Sun Dance an annual event. In the nineteenth century, however, a Crow Sun Dance was sponsored by a man seeking vengeance upon an enemy who had killed a close relative, and thus several years might pass between dances. In a circular enclosure, the sacred doll was fastened to a central pole. While they circled the pole, sometimes fasting and thirsting for several days, the dancers kept their eyes fastened on the doll as they prayed for a vision. Sometimes they practiced self-sacrifice by running skewers through their skin; sometimes they collapsed from exhaustion, only to rise and dance again when they found the strength.

The central figure of the ceremony, the Sun Dance doll, is another being created in response to a dream or vision. An account of this doll states that it was always made by young men who had first purified themselves.[14] The sewing had to be done with the sinew of the white-tailed deer, and before each stitch was taken, four songs were sung. The doll was stuffed with sacred sweet grass and pine needles. Owl feathers were attached to the body, for the owl is a sacred bird that can see at night and reveal hidden things. The design, painted with a chewed birch twig, was intended to duplicate the appearance of the doll as it had been seen in the dream. Since each dream is different, no two Sun Dance dolls look precisely alike.

The Sun Dance is still today an important ceremony for many Plains peoples. Another religious movement, a hundred years ago, is exemplified in an unusual pair of Ghost Dancers from South Dakota (figure 60), dolls that may have been made when memories of the Ghost Dance religion were still fresh. This messianic movement, inspired by the vision of a Paiute prophet named Wovoka, swept through the Plains in the 1880s, a time of cultural turmoil. The buffalo were virtually gone; settlers were fencing in the plains; and the Indians were being moved to reservations and pressured to

Figure 60. These dolls represent participants in the Ghost Dance. Although they were collected at the Sioux reservation of Pine Ridge, South Dakota, the woman's dress and both pairs of moccasins are Cheyenne in style. There was considerable intermarriage at Pine Ridge in the early 1900s, and a Cheyenne woman married to a Sioux man may have made the dolls. The male doll's shirt bears a star and crescent, a sun, hailstones, and a bald eagle. His leggings have dragonfly designs, while his face is painted with blue lightning. The woman's dress shows stars and crescents, lightning, a bald eagle, and a magpie. Her hair is made of buffalo hair. The porcupine-quill earrings represent the long earrings of dentalium shell worn on the Plains. These dolls are rich in accurate detail, and the person who made them may well have seen or participated in a Ghost Dance. *9/7607* [man], *9/7608* [woman]

give up their old ways. Wovoka's dream was of a time before strangers came to the West, and his followers hoped that if all the people prayed, dressed in special clothing, and danced the traditional Round Dance, the old days would come back.

Wovoka's vision swept through the Plains from one tribe to the next. Everywhere people began practicing the Ghost Dance, so called because of the expectation that the dead would be resurrected. They sang special songs and dressed in clothing with symbolic designs that, among the Sioux, were intended to repel enemy bullets.

The Ghost Dance movement ended tragically in 1890 at Wounded Knee, South Dakota, when U.S. Army soldiers massacred a Sioux band of nearly 300 men, women, and children who were performing the dance. The episode marked the end of a chapter in Plains history and lives on in the memories of Indian people today.

The Sioux Ghost Dance dolls may have been created by a woman who remembered the Ghost Dance days, for the designs on the clothing and faces are not only highly specific and detailed but also are ethnographically accurate. The motifs on Ghost Dance clothing were inspired by individual dreams or visions, but the same elements appeared throughout the Plains in a pan-tribal vision of the apocalypse. The sun, the stars, the crescent moon, dragonflies, bald eagles and magpies, and lightning and hailstones became Ghost Dance symbols.

Dolls such as the Sun Dance figure, the Tree Dweller, and the Health Guardian are made and used by ordinary individuals. Shamans and other religious specialists also make dolls as part of their spiritual equipment. They are generally used only by the person who controls their powers and are sometimes seen as having lives of their own.

Eskimo shamans used dolls carved of wood, bone, or ivory to represent spirit helpers (figure 61). Some observers have suggested that shamans used only wooden dolls and destroyed them after use, but others maintain that ivory figures with carved designs on the body are also shamans' dolls. Eskimo shamans, like their Siberian counterparts, were believed to make magical journeys under the sea or to the moon, and they could send their dolls on similar quests. Some Eskimo dolls were believed to be able to speak, in a language only the shaman could understand. Still others could move about unaided. A West Greenland tale, relating how the Eskimos killed a group of Old Norse settlers hundreds of years ago, claims that it was a shaman's wooden doll that revealed the hiding place of the Norse chief.[15]

Shamans' dolls are reported throughout northwestern North America, among the Carrier, Eyak, Coeur d'Alene, and Tlingit. A great Tlingit shaman named Tek ic was reported in the mid-nineteenth century to have a small doll that, by force of his powers, he could make dance on top of a drum.

From the Aleutians comes an enigmatic report of "idols who became living and had to be killed."[16] Tanaina shamans were described as using "devil dolls," small wooden figures believed to come alive at night while people slept and to stop moving at the first light of dawn. The dolls were used to extract the evil spirit from a sick person. As the shaman danced to the accompaniment

Figure 61. Eskimo shamans used wooden dolls both in curing rituals and in ceremonies intended to bring success in hunting. This one has eyes inlaid with ivory and is dressed in seal gut, which shamans themselves often wore while performing. *5/9835*

Figure 62. The charms and ornaments on this 19th-century Tanaina medicine doll from Cook Inlet, Alaska, reflect exchanges with the many foreign visitors to 18th-century Alaska, and include objects from China, Russia, France, and Connecticut. *10/6091*

of a drum, he would thrust the doll at the patient. It was believed to disappear into the patient's body and remove the sickness. Tanaina shamans were often wealthy men who displayed their riches and prestige by wearing wide belts decorated with glass trade beads and Pacific Coast dentalium shells. The Tanaina medicine doll from Cook Inlet, Alaska, wears such a belt and may represent a replica of its owner (figure 62).

During the eighteenth and nineteenth centuries, Cook Inlet was a fur-trading region visited by sailing ships from all over the world, and the charms and ornaments on the Tanaina doll reflect in microcosm the foreign currents that touched North Pacific shores. The beads come from China and Europe, probably by way of Russia. One of the "coins" is a copy of a French gaming token, the equivalent of Monopoly money, of a type made in France and Germany during the seventeenth and eighteenth centuries.[17] Another, marked "Treble gelt, St. Petersburg," appears to be a Russian equivalent. The button, from an American officer's uniform, was manufactured by the Waterbury Button Company of Connecticut (now Scoville Manufacturing).[18] The cartridge shell casing, marked "S&W," was probably made in the factories of Smith and Wesson. The doll is also adorned with the teeth and lower jawbone of a baby caribou, of the type used on Eskimo women's belts.[19] Other metal objects include a hand-cut miniature saw and a knife carried in a sheath on the back. From the back of the belt hangs an enigmatic piece, a small square metal plate darkened with age. It may be simply another object representing wealth and prestige, but it is also suggestive of a shaman's mirror, an object used by Sino-Manchurian shamans to see the souls of the dead, or to "see the world," in the same way that a fortune-teller uses a crystal ball.

Not only North American shamans used dolls in their practices. Kuna shamans of Panama use wooden figures to cure sickness by instructing the doll to locate and return the lost soul of the afflicted. These dolls are carved from various kinds of wood and named accordingly, as each type of wood is believed efficacious for a particular illness. They serve as the shaman's helpers, imbued with magical power: during a curing ritual the shaman places a number of them around the patient and calls upon them while singing and reciting. Sometimes the shaman's presence is not deemed necessary; in such a case the doll will be "rented out" and taken home to effect a cure.

Some Kuna curing dolls are very large, three or four feet tall, and are made for the rare occasions when an entire village may be stricken by an epidemic. Such a curing requires an eight-day ceremony and the use of up to several hundred figures, which are burned after use.[20] In some areas, the dolls are saved from one ritual to the next, while in others they are discarded after one use.

Figure 63. This Kuna curing doll from Panama was used by a healer in a ritual designed to cure the "loss of soul" that was believed to cause disease. He is dressed as a European doctor, possibly because European medicine was believed to be particularly efficacious. *11/4828*

Children are allowed to rescue them from the trash heap and use them as toys, for their magical powers were dissipated in the ceremony, and they are no longer sacred objects.

Clearly, Kuna curing dolls are made in enormous numbers and, if they were not composed of so perishable a material as wood, their accumulation in household trash heaps over time would be considerable. The question has been raised whether the large numbers of clay figures in archaeological sites in the same area may have served a similar purpose (see *From the Past*).

Some curing dolls, like the one illustrated in figure 63, are dressed in European clothing, while others wear Native dress. The use of foreign clothing may be intended to replicate the appearance of a European doctor who might have powerful medicines not available to the Kuna shaman. Virtually all the dolls, in both Native and European dress, wear some kind of hat, possibly signifying magical power.

As the Kuna shamans use dolls to cure illness, so shamans of the neighboring Choco people use them to keep illness and bad fortune away. In an interesting parallel with some North American groups, Choco shamans "feed" their dolls before the beginning of a ritual, placing before each one a miniature dish of food. The dolls are used primarily in two rituals: during the consecration of a batch of freshly brewed *chicha*, or maize beer, several dolls are placed near the chicha trough to ward off evil spirits; and during the dedication of an infant, the baby is presented with a guardian spirit in the form of a small wooden doll. The doll acts as a temporary home for the spirit, but with completion of the ritual the doll ceases to be sacred and can be played with like any other toy. Again, the underlying idea seems to center on the prevention of evil fortune rather than focusing on the curing process.

In some agricultural areas, shamans use their unique abilities not only for curing, divination, and love magic, but also for controlling the weather and ensuring the production of good crops. Otomi shamans of Mexico use "paper dolls" to accomplish all these purposes. The "paper dolls" are actually figures cut from *amatl*, a paper made from the inner bark of a fig tree.

Amatl has been made in central Mexico for at least 2,000 years and was used by the Aztecs for their codices, or books. They also used paper in religious observances. The sixteenth-century Spanish chronicler, Fray Bernardino de Sahagun, recorded that before Aztec traveling merchants left on a dangerous mission they cut sheets of paper into banners and painted on them pictures of the gods. The sheets of paper were laid in piles and sprinkled with the blood of a quail as a sacrificial offering.[21]

In the mountains of eastern Mexico in a number of remote villages, these ancient customs persist among the Otomi and their neighbors.

Figure 64. This Otomi paper figure from Hidalgo, Mexico, was cut from red, green, and white tissue paper by a medicine person and used in a ceremony to ensure good tomato crops. *24/2920*

The *brujo*, or healer/holy man, makes available for a fee a variety of human or human/animal shapes, each one good for a different kind of magic. Some, such as the one illustrated in figure 64, are used for specific kinds of garden magic; others are love charms or fertility medicine. Dolls used for evil spells against an enemy are cut in the shape of the devil and show the influence of Catholic teaching. Otomi paper dolls may be used at any time, but are particularly important at an annual feast, *El Costumbre*, held in honor of Moctezuma, who is believed to be the benefactor of good health and good crops. At the El Costumbre feast, the healer prepares a table upon which people place the paper cutouts of their choice. Often these paper dolls are dressed in miniature clothing. Sometimes there are so many dolls that the pile may be two inches deep. Each petitioner scatters silver coins upon the table; the healer sprinkles the blood of a chicken over the pile as a sacrifice.

Otomi paper dolls are still used today, but as this traditional society has been touched by a foreign market economy, paper dolls are now also made to sell as tourist souvenirs (see *For Purchase*). Many dolls for ritual use are made of the thin tissue paper called "papel de China" or "China paper," bought at the store. Color has become an important factor; green and yellow are preferred for the growing of corn, green and red for tomatoes. The colors of choice for the devil figures are always black and purple.

Among some agricultural peoples, such as the Pueblos of the Southwest, ritual is used to bring rain. Among the Tapirapé of central Brazil and other tribes to the east, however, shamans used dolls in a magic ceremony intended to prevent heavy rains from washing away the young corn crop. Such a doll, made of black wax, is illustrated in figure 65. These dolls represent supernatural beings called *tupan*, the helpers of Kanawana, the thunder. Tupan are believed to travel through space in small canoes made of a half gourd, and the sound of their movement through the heavens produces the noise of a storm. When the tupan shoot their arrows, they cause lightning to strike. During the Thunder Ceremony at the beginning of the rainy season, the shaman "made war" on the thunder with the assistance of the tupan figures, to prevent the rain from overpowering the freshly planted crops.

We have seen that dolls, in the widest sense of the term, have been used in a variety of religious and magical contexts by the Native peoples of the Western Hemisphere. The range of examples is by no means complete, centered as it is on a specific collection. Many types, such as the straw dolls made by the Aymara to dedicate a new house, have simply not survived to enter museum collections.

Several general statements may be made about dolls that personify spiritual beings. First, as figures of power they are used to help people grapple with forces beyond their control—illness and death, unrequited love, knowledge of the future, human fertility, and the need for food, both animal and vegetable.

Second, dolls may be temporary or permanent repositories of power. In many of the North American dolls, the power is ever present, and the dolls are considered to be highly charged with sacredness at all times. Such dolls only appear on appropriate occasions when their power is activated; otherwise they are kept hidden away. Dolls as temporary repositories of power are more characteristic of Central and South America. Many dolls are discarded once they have accomplished their purpose. This concept may explain why Otomi paper dolls, the Aymara Ekeko, and some wooden dolls from Amazonia are freely sold to tourists, while shamans' dolls from the Northwest Coast, for example, were never made for sale. They were released to foreign hands either because of a conversion to Christianity or because they were part of the equipment of a shaman who had died and no one remained who could claim his power.

Third, dolls as power figures seem to be divisible into those serving many purposes and those having a highly specific use. The dolls of the Eastern Woodlands of North America, for example, seem to have been employed in a variety of contexts: love medicine dolls could also be used as a demonstration of a Juggler's abilities, Health Guardian figures were used not only to cure a specific illness but also to bring general good health, and Tree Dwellers foretold the future and could bring luck in hunting. But the dolls used by Kuna shamans are made of a particular wood for a particular illness and seldom reused; the Otomi dolls are shaped quite specifically, even differing in whether they would bring good corn or tomato crops; and the miniature objects used to adorn the Ekeko figure are chosen with great care to answer specific wishes.

Dolls used as figures of magical and spiritual power are only one element of the profound and complex religions of the Native peoples of the Americas. But in their great variety and their richness of ethnographic detail such dolls present, in miniature, a vast universe of spiritual belief.

Figure 65. This Tapirapé figure from Brazil represents a *tupan*, a supernatural helper of Kanawana, the thunder. A tupan is described as being covered with white hair, represented here by down glued to the body of the figure. The tupan wears a headdress made from the feathers of tropical birds; the eyes are of shell. *23/3997*

FOR PERFORMANCE

THE ARTS OF PERFORMANCE—song, dance, storytelling, and poetry recital—are deeply embedded in the human consciousness, and are indeed abilities that help make us human. Performance can be simple or elaborate, an individual mime or a group dance. Performance may be for religious and spiritual observance, for fun and pleasure, or perhaps for competition, even competition for prizes. But all performances have in common the presence of an audience—an audience that may consist of other people, of animals or plants, of unseen spirits, or of gods.

Dolls and doll-like figures such as puppets and marionettes are used in performances throughout the world, including the Americas. Puppets and marionettes are manipulated in dramatic reenactments of tribal stories and legends. Dolls are used as theatrical props or as components of dance regalia. Still other dolls—past and present—are dressed and posed as performers and are made to teach children, to preserve family or community memories, or to represent a cultural practice to a non-Native audience.

In some parts of the Americas, puppets and mechanical figures are used to amaze and amuse as part of ritual performances and social gatherings. The most varied and complex use of these figures occurs among the people of the Northwest Coast and their Yup'ik and Inupiat Eskimo neighbors to the north. Northwest Coast puppetry was part of a whole ceremonial complex, rich in drama and theatrical effects. During the dark, cold winters, people gathered in the great wooden houses to participate in feasts and rituals of many

Figure 66. These two figures were manipulated with strings to dance and perform during winter ceremonies. The marionette on the left has a plate on his chest, which opens to reveal a painted figure. The dancer on the right carries a chief's rattle in the form of Raven, the powerful culture hero of the Northwest Coast people. *8/2606* [left], *6/543* [right]

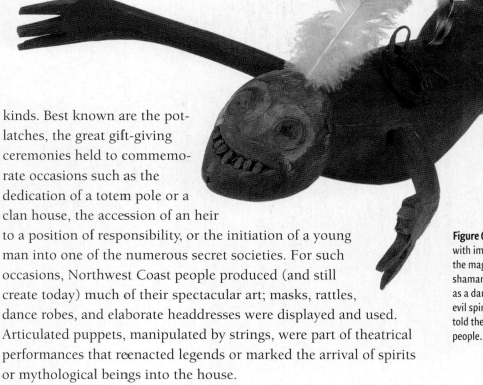

kinds. Best known are the potlatches, the great gift-giving
ceremonies held to commemorate occasions such as the
dedication of a totem pole or a
clan house, the accession of an heir
to a position of responsibility, or the initiation of a young
man into one of the numerous secret societies. For such
occasions, Northwest Coast people produced (and still
create today) much of their spectacular art; masks, rattles,
dance robes, and elaborate headdresses were displayed and used.
Articulated puppets, manipulated by strings, were part of theatrical
performances that reenacted legends or marked the arrival of spirits
or mythological beings into the house.

Figure 67. Eskimo myths are filled with imagery of flying, especially the magical flights performed by shamans. This flying figure, used as a dance ornament, represents an evil spirit named Jarneelingak who told the shaman to harm and kill people. *9/3578*

   The effects of illusion and sleight of hand were enhanced by the
darkness of the room, filled with shadows and lit only by the central fire. Puppets controlled by almost invisible strings would fly
through the air and hover in space. Others hidden in boxes buried
in the floor would appear from underground at a climactic moment,
astonishing the spectators. At some Kwakiutl potlatches, a puppet
with a detachable head danced about until a bird figure, let down
by strings from the roof, swooped down and carried away the head,
returning it later. Some Bella Coola puppets represented spirit
helpers who brought a "dead" man back to life.

   Shamans also used puppets in rituals for relieving illness. A
Tsimshian woman was cured of influenza during the 1918 epidemic
by means of a puppet made to resemble her. It was placed next to
her bed and as "all the medicine men started to sing the song of the
doll," the illness passed from the woman into the puppet, and the
patient recovered.[1]

Figure 68. This Yup´ik Eskimo dance ornament depicts a flying loon car-rying a hunter in a kayak shaped like a thresher shark. It may have been used in a performance of hunting magic, for the thresher shark is said to catch "anything he wants to." *9/3442*

Puppets on the Northwest Coast were sometimes the subject of stories. A Tsimshian legend tells of a hunter who grieved for his dead wife until he finally made a wooden marionette in her form. Its hands could be manipulated to weave, prepare food, and do all the household tasks. When some people from the village saw the marionette, they mocked the hunter for his "wooden wife," but the figure came back to life to reward him for his faithfulness.[2]

The Eskimo people of western Alaska had many dances and ceremonies intended to honor the souls of the animals that they had hunted throughout the year and to assure good hunting in the future. The dances were held in the underground ceremonial house, the *qasgiq*, where men, women, and children from the village crowded in to watch the festivities.

Whale hunting in Arctic waters was both difficult and dangerous. Ceremonies to protect the hunter and honor the spirit of the whale were powerful events that often employed mechanical figures. A four-day religious observance called "the sitting" featured figures of animals and men, some kept from year to year and others made for a specific occasion and burned after use. An observer writing in 1902 reported, "Under the shadow of the central lamp . . . were mechanical figures of diminutive men, sea parrots, and a twelve-inch wooden whale. . . . As the music played . . . the little men moved heads and arms in the same manner as the real ones."[3]

A ceremonial house at Point Hope, Alaska, had suspended above the lamp two small model umiaks with crews and hunting gear. As each man told a story of one of his past hunting adventures, the little puppet figures went through the proper motions. At Point Barrow in the 1880s, two puppets were collected for the Smithsonian: a mechanical drum player made of whale bone, wood, and caribou skin and a mechanical "kayak paddler" who could turn his head from side to side and move his arms to paddle a wooden kayak.

Some wooden figures may have been depictions of the "flying shaman," made to commemorate a shaman's magical journey to the spirit world, often said to be on the moon. Others, used as dance ornaments, depicted various kinds of flying spirits (figures 67 and 68).

The great mid-winter Arctic ceremony known as the Messenger Feast, a time when one village played host to another by feasting and elaborate gifts, was another event when puppets were part of the festivities. On these occasions, messengers carrying special

Figure 69. A drawing of the Eagle-Wolf Dance by a Native artist, ca. 1890. Courtesy of the Smithsonian Institution National Anthropological Archives. Inv. 08719800.

Figure 70. These ivory-headed Eskimo dolls depict two Eagle-Wolf, or *nilga*, dancers from Alaska. They wear elbow-length gauntlets decorated with tiny beads to represent puffin beaks. Originally, the dolls may have worn headdresses of eagle feathers. *6/9811* [two dolls]

At a Mask Dance.

staffs traveled to neighboring villages to issue an invitation, and people crowded into the qasgiq to enjoy the dances, songs, and gift giving. Wooden puppets provided part of the entertainment. Knud Rasmussen reported that at a Messenger Feast in the 1920s on Seward Peninsula, "Midway between hosts and guests is a wooden doll . . . carved very ingeniously . . . in its hand it has a small drum of very good tone, and the whole contrivance is so made that it can move its arms and head and beat the drum when a man behind pulls certain strings. When a female guest enters, the doll turns its head towards her and sends her a sigh."[4]

In places such as Kotzebue and Point Barrow, the Messenger Feast featured a *nilga* or Eagle-Wolf Dance. A row of male dancers wearing shoulder-length gloves decorated with puffin beaks danced in unison. The soft clicking sound of puffin beaks added a rhythmic accompaniment to the drumbeats. The dolls in figure 70 depict two such dancers, wearing the long gloves still worn today by the men of King Island, Alaska, as part of their dance outfits.

Dancing, to the accompaniment of hand-held drums,

continues today to be a means of cultural affirmation as well as spiritual expression—the Yup'ik Eskimo people of southwest Alaska refer to their unique kind of masked dancing as *agayuliyararput*, or "our way of making prayers." And dolls dressed as dancers continue to be made today, sometimes in group scenes such as the tableau in figure 71. Created by Nita Hartman of the Inupiaq village of Kobuk, Alaska, and entitled *Sieyukte* (The Dance), the scene captures in miniature the energy and joy of drummers and dancers alike.

As the Eskimo people dance to honor the spirits of game animals, so the dances of the Pueblos of the Southwest are intended to bring agricultural success and spiritual harmony. The most elaborate of

Figure 71. Doll maker Eva Heffle is credited with the invention of "activity dolls," sets of figures creating a tableau from real life. Other doll artists also make activity dolls, among them Inupiaq artist Nita Hartman of Kobuk, Alaska. Hartman creates here a diorama expressing the joy and energy of dancing. The large drum (seen also in the Eagle-Wolf Dance drawing figure 69) is still used in dances today. *25/5234*

these are the various katsina dances, marked by the appearance in the villages, at certain times of the year, of powerful supernatural spirits.

In the western pueblos the number of separate and distinct katsinas is very large; the Hopi, for example, are reported to have over 250, each with its own personality, behavior, song style or call, and appearance. Most are friendly; a few are funny; and some are frightening ogres and monsters who threaten naughty children. Katsinas often carry objects that help identify them, such as yucca whips, bows, rattles, staffs, or sticks. Ogre katsinas may carry butcher knives, saws, or clubs. All of these accoutrements are faithfully rendered in carved images of katsinas called katsina dolls or *tithu* in Hopi. These small figures constitute a detailed visual record of the powerful beings who are such an important part of Pueblo life.

For the Hopi, the first katsina dance of the year is Powamuy, or the Bean Dance, which takes place in February (see figures 72, 73, 74, and 75). During preparations for Powamuy, beans are sprouted in the warm, moist air of the underground ceremonial houses called kivas. During the sixteen days of Powamuy, the chief katsinas appear in the villages to dance, along with lieutenants, clowns, ogres, and others. The frightening ogres go from house to house, reminding each child of past misdeeds and failed obligations, and threatening to take the children away and eat them. As parents and relatives plead for the children's lives they hand over large quantities of food and promise that the children will be good. Finally, grumbling, the ogre-katsinas leave. The children learn from this experience the importance of proper behavior, and the fact that they can count on their families for protection. On the last day of Powamuy, the katsinas emerge from the kivas carrying freshly sprouted beans that, if growing well, promise a successful harvest in the summer ahead. Some of the bean sprouts are tied to the tithu that are given to little girls as a blessing by the various dancers.

During the growing season, the katsinas appear many other times in the village, and their dances, songs, and prayers are intended to encourage fertile growth and spiritual harmony. Finally, in July when the early corn has become ripe, the katsinas prepare to return to their mountain home. During the home dance, called Niman, people offer thanks to the katsinas by sprinkling them with corn meal, and the katsinas again provide gifts, including tithu, as part of their ritual.

Figure 72 and 73. Pictured on this page is a carved Hopi figure representing Koyaala, a clown who performs during the interludes between katsina dances and who enforces proper behavior on the part of the spectators. Opposite is a Hopi katsina called Kokosori whose body is blackened with corn smut and painted with spots representing kernals of all the colors of corn. *19/4087* [Koyaala], *9/994* [Kokosori]

Figure 74 and 75. These Hopi *tithu* represent two of the katsinas who appear in the villages during the Powamuy Ceremony. On this page is Angwusnasomtaqa, Crow Mother, who wears great black wings on her head. Crow Mother presides over the initiation of children into the katsina society, which takes place during Powamuy. In figure 75 (opposite) is Hu'katsina, carrying whips made of yucca leaves. *9/968* [Crow Mother], *18/6169* [Hu'katsina]

Virtually all tithu are carved from the dried roots of the water-seeking cottonwood tree. In recent years, cottonwood root has become scarce and expensive, but it is still the medium of choice. The body and head are carved from a single piece and appendages such as ears or snout added separately. The porous cottonwood root must be covered with a layer of white kaolin, or clay, before painting it. Early paints were native mineral or vegetable colors; today, acrylic paints are preferred. Most tithu are made by male relatives of the children who ultimately receive them and differ in style depending on the artist. Hopi tithu usually have costumes painted directly on the body; those from Zuni are more likely to wear miniature clothing constructed separately and attached to the wooden body.

Katsina dancers and clowns wear masks, but other Pueblo dances feature performers who are not masked. The Basket Dance, also held at the beginning of the planting season, is a petition for agricultural fertility. The woman in figure 76 depicts a Basket Dancer dressed in the style of San Juan Pueblo. Men and women dance in parallel lines during this dance. As the men sing, the women place their baskets on the ground and scrape them with notched sticks, producing a resonating accompaniment to the songs.

Figure 76. Like some contemporary katsina figures, these cloth dolls, dressed in the style of San Juan Pueblo, have a highly realistic, sculptural quality. They may have been made to sell to a collector. The woman's clothing, made of woven cotton, duplicates the clothing worn by Basket Dancers, and appears to have been made specifically for the doll rather than recycled from larger pieces of fabric. Her coiled basket is of the type actually used in the Basket Dance. The man is dressed as a Deer Dancer, with a yucca fiber crown and tiny bells on his knee bands. The attention to detail suggests that these dolls were probably created as display pieces to be admired rather than as toys. *22/9571* [woman], *22/9572* [man]

Although many dance performances throughout the Americas have a serious purpose, others were—and are—done purely for pleasure and sociability. The great performance event throughout Indian Country today is the powwow. The ancient *pauau* or *pawauog* (Algonquin words referring to a curing ceremony or a large gathering), has today been transformed into a social and cultural intertribal celebration that may include opportunities for performers to compete for cash prizes—sometimes very large prizes. As dancers perform in a variety of events—Traditional Dance, Fancy Dance, Shawl Dance, Grass Dance—they are judged not only for their expertise in movement but for the beauty of their regalia.

Dolls depicting powwow dancers in traditional clothing have, in the past half-century, become more accurate and authentic in detail. A dancer doll from the 1940s (figure 77) wears a generalized "Indian-type" outfit with beaded decoration and a roach headdress with a headband. But by the late twentieth century, powwow regalia became more and more modeled on the classic, traditional garb of the reservation period and before. And dolls reflected this change.

One of a number of remarkable Plains doll artists working today, Cecilia Fire Thunder creates in miniature the dress and accessories of women participating in the Women's Traditional Dance of the Plains powwow (figure 78). Fire Thunder, who is an Oglala Lakota public health specialist and advocate for minority groups and community partnerships, began making dolls with the intention of representing contemporary Plains Indian women. The elaborate decoration on these dolls reflects her own style of dressing. On one occasion, when Fire Thunder visited the National Museum of the American Indian and met Assistant Curator Emil Her Many Horses, he remarked, "You look exactly like one of your dolls!"

Musical and dance performances throughout Latin America reflect many of the same cultural values as their counterparts to the north—a connection with spiritual forces, agricultural abundance, marking of holy days, and all kinds of celebrations. The dances and festivals of Latin America combine old and new—pre-Columbian rituals with an overlay of Spanish Catholic tradition. The ancient Andean calendar follows the agricultural seasons and the movements of the sun, moon, and stars. The Catholic cycle of saints' days and feasts overlays these ancient patterns to produce church festivals, fiestas, events such as Ekeko's *alacitas* feast (see *For Power*),

and political holidays. Dancing is a feature of these events, always accompanied by instrumental music. Flutes and panpipes are particularly important. Some panpipes are of great size, reaching nearly to the ground, while others are tiny; often each dance costume includes a particular style of panpipe.

Costumed dancers are a regular feature of Andean festivals (figure 79). The fiesta of Carnaval, in February, is the major holiday for the *cholo* population, the half-Indian, half-Spanish people who form a distinct ethnic group in Bolivian towns. The cultural stereotype of a cholo is of a person who "puts on airs" and tries to copy European fashion and behavior. Cholo men and women are said to wear high-laced yellow shoes, which they consider a sign of luxury and distinction. Women's dresses are low-cut, with embroidered bodices and flaring skirts, copies of Spanish colonial dresses. Both men and women carry large, brightly colored handkerchiefs and display them as part of the dance costume.

Carnaval costumes portray cholos, bullfighters, buffoons of various kinds, and Indians of the interior forests. Many dancers are referred to as *kusillos* or *monos*, referring to the monkey-like cavorting and prancing that is part of the character of these dances.[5]

Some group dances are performed throughout the Aymara region. In the *ciriwanu*, each dancer, dressed in a white skirt and an ostrich-feather crown, plays an enormous panpipe with one hand and a drum with the other hand. Many dolls from the Andes that depict festival dancers are made as tourist souvenirs. Dressed in a variety of costumes and masks, they have great appeal for collectors.

Dolls that are used as performers in ceremonies as well as dolls depicting costumed dancers can communicate states of mind, desires of the heart, or the simple donning of a different persona. Within these contexts, dolls can tell stories, embody dreams, or reflect cultural realities.

Figure 79. These Aymara dolls represent Bolivian dancers who appear during Carnaval, the February festival that is the major holiday of the mestizo people of the Andean region. The doll on the left, dressed in an elephant-like mask headdress and a full-skirted coat, depicts a *mono*, the Spanish word for "monkey" used as a synonym for "clown." Monos dance and cavort in the streets during fiestas and add to the general merriment. They carry musical instruments, including panpipes and flutes, and dance to the accompaniment of music. *13/4496*

The doll on the right wears an "ostrich-feather" headdress and a dress in the style of the 17th-century Spanish colonial period. The design persists today in Carnaval attire. *13/4497*

FOR PURCHASE

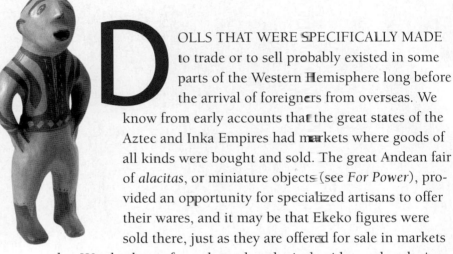

Figure 80. These dolls made by Kay Bennett carry shawls that, wrapped around the shoulders, are an important feature of traditional attire. Navajo women also display beautiful silver jewelry adorned with turquoise and other precious stones. Kay Bennett's autobiography speaks of the importance of taking care of one's jewelry so it will not "leave you to look for a better home." Jewelry was to be covered in cornmeal to keep the turquoise blue and the silver bright. *25/6988, 25/6989*

DOLLS THAT WERE SPECIFICALLY MADE to trade or to sell probably existed in some parts of the Western Hemisphere long before the arrival of foreigners from overseas. We know from early accounts that the great states of the Aztec and Inka Empires had markets where goods of all kinds were bought and sold. The great Andean fair of *alacitas*, or miniature objects (see *For Power*), provided an opportunity for specialized artisans to offer their wares, and it may be that Ekeko figures were sold there, just as they are offered for sale in markets today. We also know from the archaeological evidence that during certain periods in the Mesoamerican and Andean states small figures made in molds were mass-produced in vast quantities. Some of them show signs of use and wear while others are relatively untouched, suggesting that they were made for a variety of purposes. Whatever their use, the fact that they were mold-made in such large numbers suggests an enterprise engaged in by specialists who may have been supported by their production. Aztec records mention an annual festival day for the makers of dolls, possibly the forerunners of the contemporary toy makers who create dolls to make a living.

Throughout Mexico and Central America, toy makers have always been artisans working in their own homes, often in charge of a family enterprise that includes parents, children, cousins, and grandparents as participants in production. The mold-made papiermâché dolls produced for sale today in Guanajuato, Mexico, are the work of such an industry; the molds are handed down from father to son (figure 81). The doll makers produce the arms, legs, and

torso by pressing wet, shredded paper into the molds, removing the forms after they dry, and gluing the front and back pieces together. The clay puppets from archaeological sites, made the same way, were "glued" together with wet clay.

Craftwork in Mexico has always been highly localized, with certain towns and *municipios* being known for special kinds of work. The town of Salamanca, in Guanajuato, for example, is the place to buy stringed wooden puppets. Ocotlan, in Oaxaca, is the center of production for pottery bells made in the shape of women with long skirts. Dolls and animals constructed of tule reeds are to be found in Jalisco. Aguascalientes is where *charamusca* is made, the sweet yellow taffy formed into doll shapes and eaten all during Holy Week.

Some dolls, especially those made for major religious holidays, become widely available for a brief time, such as small figures made for Christmas crèche scenes, or the papier-mâché dolls depicting devils and Judases that are sold at Easter time. According to Donald Cordry, children play with Judas dolls throughout Holy Week, until

Figure 81. This type of papier-mâché jointed doll has been called "the best-known doll in Mexico." Made in Guanajuato, it comes in many sizes and always has a name painted on the front such as Flor, Lola, or Rafaelija. Brightly painted and wearing glittering painted-on jewelry, these dolls are described as being dressed like circus performers. *25/2194*

Good Friday, after which the dolls go up in the smoke of a central bonfire.[1] Skeleton dolls are made for the November festival of the Day of the Dead. Some of them have a wire spring in the neck or joints so they can be made to dance. Many of these dolls, made today for a Catholic ritual calendar, have roots in an ancient yearly religious cycle, one that predates the first arrival of Spanish missionaries. And, today, the intense interest in folk art and the greater ease of travel and communication means that dolls from Mexico are available in markets worldwide and throughout the year.

Dolls from Central and South America were always low in price, making it economically feasible for middlemen to resell them at a profit. By the mid-twentieth century, the rise in tourism and the development of world markets stimulated the demand for all kinds of indigenous crafts, dolls among them. Acquiring and marketing merchandise half a century ago, before the development of local craft cooperatives and the Internet, posed logistical problems that challenged all but the most dedicated and determined merchants. One well-documented entrepreneurial model was the Kimports Company of Independence, Missouri, which sold dolls from all over the world for more than fifty years, beginning in the 1930s. Their newsletter, *Doll Talk*, described in a chatty, informal fashion trends in the doll collectors' market and lists of what was currently available through mail order.

Dolls from the Americas were a small but steady portion of their business from the beginning. The company was limited only by the difficulty of finding dependable sources, for dolls tended to be made sporadically or seasonally, and buyers needed to be on the scene at the appropriate moment. Kimports agents visited consulates, government-sponsored craft organizations, co-ops, tribal councils, and even mission churches in their efforts to locate doll makers. A 1962 newsletter reported that they had received a shipment of dolls from Ecuador made by the members of a mission church as a fundraiser.[2] In the 1960s, a source in Bolivia managed to supply them with dolls made by prisoners in La Paz, who produced them "in exchange for cigarette money."[3] A description of one of the Bolivian dolls resembles the Carnaval doll in figure 79: ". . . leather hands with separated fingers, costumes of red, yellow, blue, gray, and white felt . . . blue and gray felt masks topped with five vertical cylinders. . . ."[4]

One perennial favorite offered by Kimports was the pair of Quechua dolls shown in figure 82. The catalogue describes them as having "classic Inca heads . . . cloth bodies rather strangely proportioned and utterly delightful costumes of roughly loomed llama hues."[5]

Kimports used not only their own agents but also individual traders, some of whom resorted to barter rather than cash. A steady supplier in British Guiana (Belize) reported in 1944 that no more wax or rubber dolls would be available unless the company could send down some small beads. According to the newsletter, the beads were sent and the dolls were once more offered for sale.[6] A Panama trader bought five wooden dolls from "some kids in San Blas who were playing with them."[7] He paid twenty-five cents each for three balsa and two mahogany dolls, dressed in the appliquéd shirts called *molas*.

One of the Kimports staples was dolls from Guatemala, such as the woman in figure 83. For $1.25 each, one could order a male or female doll with "most charming hand loomed cotton garments; papa totes a big market-day crate, while mamma balances about as much merchandise on her head, carrying precocious looking junior in a shoulder sling."[8] The quality of workmanship on these dolls is not stinted, despite the low prices. The doll illustrated wears a skirt of dark blue and white *morga* cloth, dyed with indigo and woven in a plaid design specific to its village of origin. Some male dolls wear carefully made miniature straw hats. Another type represents a weaver sitting at a loom working on a length of half-woven fabric.

Another type of Guatemalan doll, handled by Kimports but still widely available elsewhere, is a set of six tiny figures called "trouble dolls," made of brightly colored thread wound around a wire armature. The printed legend states that each doll is to be removed from the box at bedtime and told of a particular worry. During the night, it is said, the doll will solve the problem. The most recent shipment of these dolls at a large museum gift shop referred to them as "Therapy ™ Dolls," probably to increase their appeal to a contemporary market. "Trouble dolls," packaged in a small bentwood box decorated with painted designs, were sold in the 1960s for one dollar; today's price is still very low.

Dolls have been offered for sale in the markets of Latin America perhaps for as long as markets have existed. The picture in North America was different; although there were trading networks throughout the continent, there were no central markets, and dolls were not produced as commodities. But with the arrival of large numbers of foreigners in the seventeenth and eighteenth centuries, the picture began to change. The age of European expansion brought an increasing interest in cultural exotica from all over the world. As explorers, traders, missionaries, and government officials fanned out through the hemisphere, they sought to bring home what they called "artificial curiosities" as souvenirs of their travels. By the nineteenth century, curio cabinets had become part of the furnishings of upper-class and middle-class English and European houses. From London to Leningrad, from Boston to Berlin, the first ethnographic museums were beginning to be established to display objects made by "the other"—inhabitants of strange and distant places.

As objects evocative of different cultures, dolls and forms of miniature doll equipment were ideal. Small and easily carried, recognizable but foreign, they had a cozy familiarity combined with an irresistibly exotic appearance appealing not only to individual collectors but also to museums, where their finely detailed clothing and ornament made them rich sources of ethnographic information.

How dolls became established objects of commerce varied from one Native group to the next, for each group had its own lifeways and its own reaction to the effects of foreign contact. Over the years, the process appears to have had three broad, overlapping strands: first, as a lagniappe or byproduct of other kinds of trade; then the deliberate production of dolls specifically produced as curios and souvenirs; and finally both the careful replication of older traditional forms and the creation of contemporary art forms for a specialized collectors' market.

Figure 83. Small dolls with bodies made of cloth or of wire covered with twisted paper are produced throughout Mexico and Central America, often by artisans working at home. Many of them are dressed in hand-woven textiles in traditional style. This Guatemalan woman with a broom wears a *huipil* (blouse) and a skirt of indigo-dyed *morga* cloth. She carries a baby in a *tzut*, the all-purpose cloth that serves for every use from scarf to market bag. *22/3685*

Figure 84. Mapuche weavers of Chile are known for making beautifully woven saddle blankets, which are carried to market piled high on the back of a horse. The riders perch on top of the blankets as seen here. *17/6662*

Figure 85. This Ojibwe trio, named "Nokomis"(left), "Hiawatha" (center), and "Minnehaha" (right), in tribute to Longfellow's beloved poem, presents a romanticized version of Indian people, made familiar through Hollywood movies and popular literature. Their clothing—created from cut-up kid gloves—leans heavily on the Plains for inspiration, but the beadwork, the leggings, and the moccasins are done in a Woodlands style. Fine examples of souvenir art, they were probably made for a non-Native market. Their names undoubtedly added sales appeal. *22/4762* [Nokomis], *22/4760* [Hiawatha], *22/4761* [Minnehaha]

The first stage, which began in the seventeenth century along the Atlantic Coast and the eighteenth century in Alaska, was a byproduct of other kinds of commerce. Dolls and other cultural artifacts were traded or sold as a casual aside to the real business of dealing in sea otter furs, beaver pelts, deer hides, and other commodities that built fortunes for European and Russian merchants. The dolls of this early period were seen by the buyers as exotic curios and by the sellers as expendable ephemera. Many shamans' dolls lost their usefulness in the wake of conversions to Christianity; children's toys were easy to replace; medicine dolls could be replicated by those who had dreamed the proper dreams. Dolls considered disposable within their own culture, such as the Kuna curing dolls, were sold instead of being tossed on the trash heap. The Bering Strait people in Alaska considered their toy dolls and other artifacts to be worthless in comparison with the metal knives and rifles that they could get in trade. E. W. Nelson, who collected dozens of dolls and other artifacts for the Smithsonian during his 1877–81 stay in Alaska, was called, "the man who buys good-for-nothing things."[9]

This early period of casual and haphazard commerce in dolls and other artifacts began to change as Native people were drawn more and more into a money economy. As the supply of furs and hides began to dwindle, other ways of making money were explored. During this next period, some groups made a conscious attempt to produce traditional dolls that could be marketed to foreign buyers. Native artisans were keenly aware of which goods would sell and which would not; dolls were only one of a number of commodities they modified to suit outside tastes. The Andean knitted dolls, made as toys for hundreds of years, were now produced with silk yarns and embellished with miniature accessories. Birchbark dolls from the Great Lakes, which had been homely, simple cutouts for children, acquired skirts, feathers, and painted faces. Katsina dolls became realistic sculptures with fine details such as musculature and fingernails clearly rendered.

Some dolls seem to have been created as a response to foreign notions of what is "Indian" and catered to romantic ideas such as those expressed in Henry Wadsworth Longfellow's popular poem *The Song of Hiawatha* (1855). The dolls in figure 85, sold with the names "Hiawatha," "Minnehaha," and "Nokomis," are exquisitely made, but conform to no specific tribal tradition. They are dressed in a generalized "Indian" style, leaning heavily on the Plains for inspiration, but the beadwork and accessories are like those made in the eastern Great Lakes area, and they combine elements designed to appeal to Western tastes.

In North America, the earliest dolls made specifically for sale were produced in the fur-trading areas of the Northwest and the Northeast. The Eskimo people of Alaska, who had always made dolls in abundance, were quick to pick up on the foreign demand for them and made not only traditional dolls but also small models such as dolls in kayaks. These were often quite realistically created of animal gut or hide with miniature fittings of ivory or wood.

In 1794, Peter Puget, a member of George Vancouver's expedition to the Pacific Northwest, acquired several kayak models and wrote that "these people . . . were well provided, in expectation of finding a profitable market. . . ."[10] The Museum of Anthropology and Ethnography in St. Petersburg has thirty-two model kayaks, all collected before 1850, presumably during the peak period of the fur trade. The Aleut people participated in this commerce as well by creating small *baidarkas*, the three-man kayaks used in the Aleutian Islands (figure 86).

Northeastern North America was another area where the production of dolls for sale began in the eighteenth century. Miniature dolls and equipment had long been made for use in medicine bundles, and it was an easy transition to begin producing them for sale. Some of these miniatures, now in European museums, are finely crafted dolls as well as canoes, snowshoes, bows and arrows, and guns. One model, in the Pitt-Rivers Museum in Oxford, England, even includes a tiny wampum belt. The Horniman Museum in London houses a pair of eighteenth-century English wooden dolls dressed as Cree women of eastern Canada.[11] The detail is exquisite, even including intricate wrapped quillwork on the fringes of the dresses.

The Huron people also participated in this market, creating beautifully detailed dolls as exemplars of Native life. One family group, documented as having been collected at the Huron village of Lorette in 1788, incorporates clothing adorned with quillwork, glass beads, and silk ribbon obtained in trade. The Huron trapper in winter clothing was a familiar figure in the forests of Quebec (figure 87). Dressed in a *capote*, or coat with a pointed hood, and

Figure 86. These Aleut sea otter hunters in a three-man *baidarka* wear the painted bentwood hats used to minimize sun glare on the open water. The hats were not only symbols of prestige but were also meant to be aesthetically pleasing to the sea otter, an animal that the hunters believed to have delicate sensibilities, which would be enticed by beautiful things. Drawings of baidarkas by 18th-century visitors to the Arctic are strikingly similar to this little model. *16/8275*

equipped with snowshoes, he spent the winter following his own trap lines as well as guiding commercial trappers into the interior along the rivers and streams. Of all the curios taken home by visitors to Canada, the trapper doll with his equipment was among the most popular.

The neighboring Iroquois people, especially those who lived in the vicinity of the great tourist center of Niagara Falls, also made souvenirs for sale. By the nineteenth century, railroad excursions to the falls brought in thousands of visitors, all of whom wanted something "genuine Indian" to take home. Mark Twain wrote of the shops at Niagara Falls being filled with "dainty Indian beadwork, stunning moccasins, and equally stunning toy figures."[12]

The sale of souvenirs became, for some families, an important source of income and was set up as a business. Beaded pincushions in the Victorian style were perhaps the most financially lucrative souvenirs, but cornhusk dolls were also extremely popular. They were often sold on the street, but arrangements were also made to supply storekeepers with a specified number of pieces to stock their

Figure 87. This Huron trapper wears the traditional *capote*, or coat with a pointed hood; his wife is dressed in calico trade cloth but wears the same old-style leggings seen on the Cree doll in figure 41. They were collected in 1890 at the Huron village of Lorette in Canada, a center for the production of snowshoes and moccasins in the 1890s. These dolls were presumably sold as souvenirs. The painted designs on the man's face, which are also found on certain medicine dolls, may refer to hunting medicine. *20/5053* [man], *20/5054* [woman]

shelves. Sometimes novel materials were introduced. In the 1930s, for example, corn blight struck the Tuscarora area, and cornhusks to make dolls were unobtainable. A young Tuscarora man who had on hand a supply of dyed leather offered the store manager dolls with leather heads instead, and when the manager ordered 1,000 of them, the man and his family "got a production line going" to turn out the dolls. Some women began specializing in leather heads as a variation of the standard cornhusk dolls.[13]

While artists and craftsmen in tourist areas such as Niagara Falls and Alaska marketed dolls, baskets, pottery, and pincushions to an eager public, and while companies such as Kimports acted as middlemen in a profit-making enterprise, a third movement in commoditizing Native arts—sparked by white philanthropists—began to develop at the end of the nineteenth century. It was made possible by a rising interest in collecting Indian objects to decorate the home. Many Victorian parlors featured an "Indian corner" where baskets, pottery, Navajo rugs, beaded pincushions, dolls, model totem poles, birchbark letter holders, and other souvenirs picked up on tours into Indian Country were displayed as evidence of good taste and sophistication.

Native arts of all kinds were distributed by department stores, offered through traders' catalogues, and mentioned in arts and crafts publications, often packaged in a romanticized way as a means of "selling the image" as well as the objects. Throughout the United States, Indian reform movements were developed, led by affluent upper-class women and fueled by a desire to encourage Indian women in achieving a measure of economic independence by means of arts and crafts. In 1892 Boston, the establishment of an Indian Industries League was proposed, and the Women's National Indian Association (WNIA) urged—through pamphlets, letters, and parlor talks—economic self-sufficiency for Indian women.

This social movement persisted, in some cases, well into the twentieth century, as exemplified by the experience of Deaconess Harriet Bedell and the Seminole people of Florida. The Seminole, who had moved from further north to the Everglades early in the nineteenth century, had long ago discarded their heavy buckskin clothing and replaced it with cooler and more comfortable cotton shirts made of European trade cloth in a style that was instantly recognizable as "Seminole"—and which, for men, may have been inspired by Scottish Highland clothing of the eighteenth century.[14] Women wore long, full calico skirts and short capes. By the 1880s, when hand-operated sewing machines became available, women began decorating clothing with stripes and with design bands of intricately assembled geometric patterns sewn into a long strip and inserted as a separate piece.

The Seminole had been supporting themselves by various means, not only by selling dolls and other crafts, but also by operating "Indian villages" for the benefit of tourists. In 1933, an Episcopalian Deaconess, Harriet Bedell, took it upon herself to expand the crafts program and eliminate the "Indian village" at Glade Cross Mission in the southern Everglades.[15] "Exhibit arts and crafts but not people!"

became her slogan, and she began purchasing for resale grass baskets and dolls made of palmetto fiber, the latter dressed in what had become traditional Seminole clothing (figure 88). She referred to her program as "Industrial Work," reflecting the wordage of the Boston-based Indian Industries League. She decided what was salable and what was not, offered suggestions for improvement, and screened out objects that she felt were "not Seminole," such as tomahawks, peace pipes, and the totem poles that had been made to entice visitors into the Indian camps.

Deaconess Bedell exercised strict control over the items offered for sale. The patchwork clothing on the dolls, as well as the full-size clothing, was acceptable only if it was one of seven designs she considered "traditional." She frowned on rickrack ornamentation as "tourist, not Indian," and effectively prevented the introduction of any new designs, although women had always experimented with new forms.

Marketing Seminole dolls from such a remote area was always a problem, and Bedell corresponded widely with possible outlets, including the Commissioner of Indian Affairs. During the 1950s, she often packed her car with arts and crafts and drove to New York, staying until everything was sold. She had outlets in Miami, and she also sold by mail order. The Kimports Company was apparently one of her outlets, for their newsletter reported in 1944 that the stock of Seminole dolls was dwindling because war shortages were making it impossible to get the cotton material used in making doll clothes.

Glade Cross Mission was destroyed by a hurricane in 1960, and Deaconess Bedell, then in her eighties, was unable to reactivate it. But the Seminole themselves have carried on the work she began, by supplying a now highly developed tourist market. Today, both the Seminole Tribe of Florida and the Miccosukee Tribe of Indians of Florida maintain cultural centers with gift shops where they demonstrate doll making and other arts. They supply hotel gift shops and tourist centers throughout Florida, recognizing that for many visitors a Seminole doll is the quintessential Florida souvenir. Seminole doll makers travel the powwow circuit, displaying and selling their wares to Indian and non-Indian visitors alike. The Marketplace on the tribal Website displays dolls of all sizes as well as innovative forms such as key ring decorations and tissue box covers. Although some of the larger, costlier dolls wear clothing illustrating the original patchwork style, most of them wear items

Figure 88. Seminole dolls have been produced for the tourist trade since early in the 20ᵗʰ century. This one, constructed of palmetto fiber, wears a man's "big shirt," adapted from a 19ᵗʰ-century European style. The loose fit and long sleeves provide both coolness and protection from Everglades mosquitos. *22/1549*

trimmed with rickrack, like the clothing worn by the Seminole themselves.

The Eastern Band Cherokee people of North Carolina, whose reservation adjoins the Great Smoky Mountains National Park, also developed craft programs, and dolls are among the many products offered. The wooden doll in figure 89 wears a Cherokee version of an eighteenth- or early nineteenth-century European dress, a style traditional for the Cherokee for 200 years. In 1973, the Kimports catalogue offered, for $12.50 each, three dolls depicting people important in Cherokee history. They were modeled after characters from an annual pageant reenacting the Trail of Tears, the episode in the 1830s when many Cherokee people were forcibly removed from their eastern homes to settle in Oklahoma. The dolls offered included Sequoyah, inventor of the Cherokee alphabet; Sarah, a girl enrolled in a female seminary; and a man called The Villager, who was dressed in the fashion of the 1830s.

The newsletter recommended these dolls to collectors as "representing an unforgettable segment of American history."[16] The creation of these character dolls, modeled after particular people and with careful attention to historical accuracy, was a precursor to the specialized collectors' market that thrives today.

And as another form of contemporary marketing, Cherokee dolls are today available through the Quallah Arts and Crafts Mutual of North Carolina, a cooperative founded by the Eastern Band of the

Figure 89. This carved wooden doll wears a Cherokee version of an 18th- or early 19ᵗʰ-century European dress, a style traditional to the Cherokee for 200 years. Today the Cherokee produce dolls, pottery, baskets, and woven sashes in a crafts revival that has become an important source of income. *20/9729*

Cherokee tribe; by the Cherokee Indian Tribe of South Carolina (ECSIUT); and by the United Keetoowah Band of Cherokee Indians of Oklahoma. Each of these groups also maintains a Website where dolls are offered "subject to availability." A number of talented doll makers, including Hank Orr and Richard and Berdina Crowe, have created dolls that are much sought after by collectors.

In the southwestern United States, a market for Indian arts and crafts, including dolls, developed in the late nineteenth century, when the first railroads were constructed. The Southern Pacific Railroad crossed Arizona in 1877; the Santa Fe came into New Mexico a year later. The arrival of travelers for business or pleasure created a demand for Indian wares that was to reach a crescendo by the turn of the century. Each "jerkwater stop" along the way, where trains stopped to replenish water, also became a place where travelers could alight to view the sights and buy souvenirs. Fred Harvey made a fortune by building a restaurant at each watering stop and stocking it with goods for sale made by the local people. Craft workers also met the trains and sold their wares directly. Rugs, pottery, baskets, and silverwork were being discovered by collectors and used as decorations in their homes. The production of new forms of dolls was a part of this burgeoning market.

The Yuma and Mohave people of the lower Colorado River and the Mohave Valley began producing small clay dolls sometime after the mid-nineteenth century and, by the 1880s, selling them regularly to travelers. Representing men, women, children, and infants in cradleboards (figure 90), these dolls give us a detailed look at dress and ornament of the period. Yuma women, for example, characteristically tattooed their chins with lines and parallel rows of dots, while both sexes practiced body painting. Although traditional female clothing consisted of a willow bark skirt with a belt of cord, European trade cloth was substituted as soon as it became available. Yuma and Mohave dress also featured a lavish use of beads. As early as the eighteenth century, the Yuma were showing a preference for blue and white beads in several sizes, and everyone wore chokers and earrings. Whether or not Yuma and Mohave dolls represent a continuation of a prehistoric form is still an open question. They bear some resemblance to certain pottery figures found in archaeological sites in the Southwest, but to date no direct line of descent has been established.

Figure 90. Yuma and Mohave dolls have been made for the tourist trade for more than 100 years, although they may have more ancient roots in archeological Southwestern pottery. Yuma dolls (left) have hair tucked into a depression in the head and secured with a cloth band, while Mohave dolls are known for their large noses. Both kinds of dolls wear body paint and masses of bead jewelry. *18/9720* [Yuma], *19/4106* [Mohave]

Figure 91. These two natty cowboys, standing with arms akimbo in a very Western pose, are examples of the popular caricatures of foreign visitors, as interpreted by the keen eyes and skillful hands of Pueblo potters of the late 19th century. *6/6821* [left], *15/3508* [right]

Pueblo potters in New Mexico also participated in the tourist market by making not only bowls and jars but also figurines. Some of the most popular were those produced at Cochiti beginning in the 1870s. The early examples borrowed heavily from archaeological effigy figures and displayed designs found on traditional pottery.[17] Later and more common styles (figure 91) were often self-portraits or whimsical caricatures of foreigners. Cowboys and priests were two of the most popular types.

Most people who have seen early photographs or postcards of Indian artisans flocking around a Santa Fe train continue to think of the Southwestern curio trade as a one-to-one transaction. Jonathan Batkin has pointed out, however, that the great bulk of the merchandise was sold through curio dealers in Santa Fe and by mail-order catalogue to points in the East. As one example, the Tewa Pueblo of Tesuque produced a number of figurines, particularly the small seated figures known as "Rain Gods," which were packed and

shipped one hundred to the barrel. Orders in the thousands were not unknown. At one point, the Gunther Candy Company of Chicago used these figures as a premium for the purchase of candy, and they became known throughout the country as a promotional logo for the company.

As these figures became more and more popular with the general public, they were denigrated and ignored both by serious collectors and anthropologists, who looked down on them as "tourist art." As early as 1889, an article in the *American Anthropologist* titled "The Debasement of Pueblo Art" urged that the manufacture of these forms should be discouraged and that museums should neither collect nor accept them.[18] Babcock states that in the 1930s, when the Museum of New Mexico was encouraging pottery revivals, it also discouraged the manufacture of figurines. During the early 1960s at Indian Market in Santa Fe, there was no category for figurative forms other than "Pottery, Miscellaneous," and the condescending word *mono* (in Spanish, "monkey, fool, mere doll") was used to refer to all figurines.[19]

But in the 1960s, the Cochiti potter Helen Cordero created a new form and a new market—one that is still expanding half a century later (figure 92). Cordero began with a series of "little people," men and women, and the first time she showed them, during a Santo Domingo feast day, the folk art collector Alexander Girard bought all her pieces at $7.50 each. He commissioned other pieces, including a larger seated figure with children, and Cordero responded with the first Storyteller—a depiction of her grandfather surrounded by five children.

The Storyteller was an immediate success and stimulated the production of pottery figures throughout the pueblos. In 1965, a Storyteller won first prize at Santa Fe Indian Market. By 1983, there were more than 100 potters working. "Storyteller" has become a generic form with variations such as Storyteller bears, frogs, and owls, and miniature Storytellers that are made by a few potters. There is even a Storyteller fashioned to sit on a desk and hold business cards.

Pima and Tohono O'odham basket-makers also entered the lucrative tourist market, producing coiled baskets in various forms and sizes. One innovation introduced by the Tohono O'odham was animals and human figures using a coiled basketry technique. These were usually made of white yucca with black devil's claw (*martynia*) coiled in to add detail. Most of these figures represented women with long, full skirts; male figures are relatively rare and more difficult to do. "Life form baskets" have been entered in various competitions through the years, and the one illustrated in figure 93 was exhibited at the 1960 Pima County Livestock Show.

The collectors' market for dolls from the Southwest has also affected the production of katsina dolls, or *tithu* (*tihu* in the singular). A hundred years ago tithu were simple in form, homemade in appearance, and easy for a child to grasp. They stood solidly erect on both feet, with a kind of simple dignity, often with arms held close to the body (see *For Performance*, figures 72, 73, 74, and 75). But as collectors began seeking them out, first as tourist souvenirs and later as art objects, tithu became more elaborate and more realistic, often resembling small sculptures rather than dolls. Many are carved in action poses; many are now signed by the artists (and for the first time women as well as men are katsina artists); and variations such as miniature figures and tableaus with groups have become popular.

The movement of katsina tithu into the field of contemporary art is marked by their inclusion in the annual Santa Fe Indian Market, a centerpiece for excellence in Native arts. Artists compete in two categories: traditional and contemporary. The standards are rigid. A tihu must come from the cultural tradition of the carver (i.e., only Hopi and Zuni carvers may compete); it must be carved only from the root (or for Zuni tihu, root and limbs) of the cottonwood tree; and tithu must be made only with hand tools and of traditional materials.[20] Carvers of contemporary tithu may use motorized and other tools and—with disclosure—may include decorative stone and metal elements such as beads and cabochons.

This highly codified set of standards marks a clear departure from the older, simpler tradition of creating a tihu to delight and educate a child. And there are still carvers who would never sell a tihu, likening it to "selling your children." But the artists who participate in Indian Market, although they may be schooled in a tradition of studio art, are nevertheless culturally grounded in the ancient and profound knowledge of the power and meaning of these small figures. The same cannot be said of all tihu carvers. The popularity of katsina dolls in the commercial market has led to abuses such as cheap, inaccurate copies made by non-Native carvers, even

Figure 93. Pima and Tohono O'od-ham basket-makers began producing basketry dolls in the 1930s, using traditional techniques and materials. This figure, made of white yucca and black devil's claw (*martynia*), was made to sell at the 1960 Pima County Livestock Show. *22/9077*

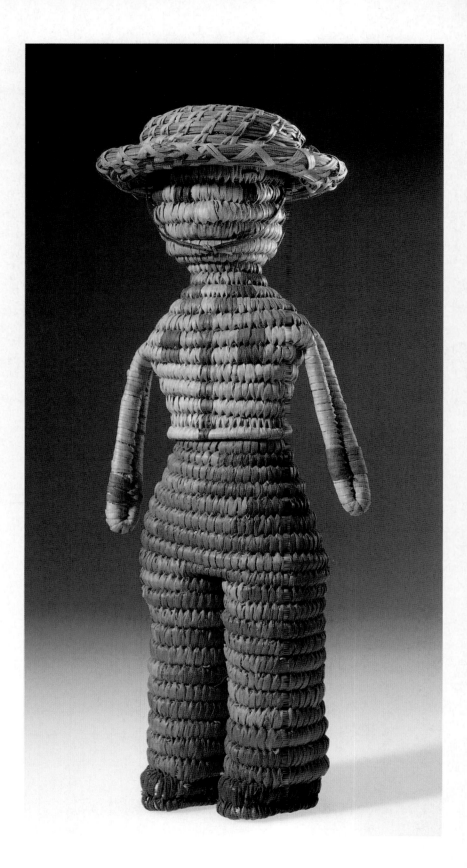

Figure 94. Dawa, the katsina representing the sun, seldom appears in the public dances in the pueblos. But because his appearance is so striking, with a large painted mask surrounded by feathers, he is a popular subject with carvers and a favorite with collectors. The border around the sun is traditionally fashioned from braided cornhusks into which eagle feathers are inserted. Here the artist, Story Huma (Hopi), used rickrack to achieve the braided effect. Dawa carries a rattle in the right hand and a flute in the left hand. *25/5576*

Figure 95. Each pueblo has its own version of Koshare, the painted clown; this one is from First Mesa. During the katsina dances, groups of clowns act rowdy, make fun of visitors, and present an example of how *not* to behave. One young Hopi woman remembers her father cautioning her, "Don't give them any fodder," and she recalls trying hard to stand quietly so as not to call attention to herself. Koshare are always hungry and are particularly fond of watermelons. A favorite game is playing "toss and catch" with a watermelon, gradually moving apart until someone drops the melon and it breaks open—whereupon everyone has a feast. *25/5588*

carvers from foreign countries such as Japan. Some figures are mass-produced in white-owned factories that employ workers who may be Native but who are neither Hopi nor Zuni—the only peoples with a cultural connection with katsinas. As a marketing ploy, the products of these factories may truthfully be described as "Indian-made," and because they are mass-produced and cheaper than genuine katsina dolls, they are widely sold, even in some museum shops.

From the beginning we have seen the commoditization of dolls take many forms, among them a simple one-on-one trade or purchase of a worn-out toy or ritual object; the creation of dolls specifically fashioned to appeal to a foreign buyer; and a market-driven, opportunistic strategy by white middlemen (such as Kimports) or by philanthropic outside brokers such as Deaconess Bedell.

Of all the public and private efforts to market Indian arts, dolls among them, the most ambitious and wide-ranging was a federal program established during the Great Depression, the Indian Arts and Crafts Board (IACB). Created by Franklin D. Roosevelt's New Deal in 1935, the IACB's mission was the encouragement and support of Indian arts as a means of economic development for Native people. Under the leadership of John Collier and his general manager Rene D'Harnoncourt, the IACB worked with public and private agencies throughout the United States to encourage the development of craft programs for economic development. During the 1939 Golden Gate Exposition in San Francisco and in 1941 at the Museum of Modern Art in New York City, exhibitions of historic and contemporary Native work also presented Indian artists demonstrating the creation of dolls and other crafts.

One of the IACB initiatives was the creation of regional Native crafts organizations, some of which have been mentioned and many of which are still in existence today—among them the Alaska Native Arts and Crafts Association, the Seminole Craft Center, the Oklahoma Indian Arts and Crafts Cooperative, and the Qualla (North Carolina) Arts and Crafts Mutual. Doll making was one of the activities promoted as a means of increasing family income. With the encouragement of high-quality dolls marketed to collectors, IACB also for the first time encouraged the emergence of the named artist. Among the first doll makers to gain such recognition were the previously mentioned Richard and Berdina Crowe of the Eastern

Figure 96. The Kotzebue artist Ethel Washington (Inupiat name Agnakluwak) created highly realistic portrait dolls with heads whittled from birch wood and miniature clothing remarkable for its authenticity and careful attention to detail. The woman in this pair displays a chin tattoo, a mark of adulthood, and carries two of her "trademark" pieces, a birchbark berry basket and a berry scoop. Washington made the miniature tools, including the hunter's bow. *25/5302* [man], *25/5301* [woman]

Band of Cherokee and Ethel Washington, Inupiaq artist of Kotzebue, Alaska. Washington was only one of what is today a large number of talented Eskimo doll makers, but she was perhaps the earliest, working from the 1930s until her death in 1967.[21] She specialized in husband-wife-infant families dressed in accurately replicated fur clothing and carrying appropriate gear—a bark basket for the woman and a hunting spear or bow for the man (figure 96).

In 1960, the IACB successfully pushed for the creation of the Institute of American Indian Arts in Santa Fe, New Mexico, a school open to young Indian artists from the entire United States. Students at the school work in studios that may be far from home, and they learn, along with artistic techniques, methods of marketing their work. Graduates, along with other contemporary doll makers, have moved far from the old stereotypes of selling their creations to a stranger on a train. The creation and marketing of Indian dolls today, at the beginning of a new millennium, continues to evolve into new forms, new uses, and new artistic and cultural expressions.

A few examples will suffice. One of the phenomena that have occurred since the 1960s is the increased energy among Native people in acknowledging, preserving, and asserting their cultural heritage. Many tribes have developed and are building cultural centers and museums not only as a means of teaching their own children about tribal traditions but also as a way of presenting themselves to outside visitors. Making dolls in traditional clothing and selling them by various means (museum shops, mail order catalogues, tribal Websites) serves both as an income-generator and an educational tool. Interestingly, little girls have always learned, from mothers or grandmothers, the tools and techniques for making clothing (see *For Playing*). In the world today, such knowledge may have to be re-learned by adults who talk with community elders and who study old garments in museum collections in order to replicate them. Such efforts are making possible the revitalization of traditional cultures everywhere.

There are doll artists such as Stephen Chrisjohn (Oneida) who have taken a traditional form—in his case the Iroquois cornhusk doll—and refined it into a miniature, sculptured form. His "hunter" (figure 97), dressed in leather adorned with glass beads, carries a tiny hunting knife with a sterling silver blade and an ivory handle, an artistic statement that goes far beyond any kind of "souvenir art."

Figure 97. This exquisitely detailed Oneida hunter, made by Steven Chrisjohn, carries arrows with tiny stone points hafted with sinew. His hunting knife has a sterling silver blade and an ivory handle. *25/9271*

Some doll artists incorporate humor or social commentary into their work. Among them are Rosalie Paniyak, Cup'ik Eskimo from Alaska, whose Statue of Liberty with a fur torch and a seal gut over-dress brings a touch of whimsicality to a piece of monumental solemnity (figure 99). Yet another example of whimsy is Oneida artist Judi Jourdan's blonde "lady in a bikini," a rag doll that calls up echoes of the nineteenth-century Cochiti figures that poked fun at the white visitors who came to the Southwest.

Other artists use dolls to express an idea larger than a single doll form. Some Inupiat Eskimo doll artists create tableaus such as a group of dancers (figure 71) or a basket-maker (figure 100) to reflect traditional life and to assert its existence today. And Lakota

Figure 98. Oneida doll artist Judi Jourdan challenges the stereotype of the rag doll with this soft sculpture of a blonde bathing beauty. A contemporary version of the "pretty ladies" of ancient Mesoamerica, this witty creation expands our concept of "Native American doll" into an entirely new and original dimension. *25/5778*

Figure 9 Rosalie Paniyak is one of a group of doll makers from Chevak, Alaska, who have developed a distinctive regional style characterized by a droll humor and charm. Although many Chevak dolls engage in everyday village activities, Paniyak has here referenced the wider world in her version of the Statue of Liberty. Titled *My Love, Miss Liberty*, the doll wears a rain-proof gut overdress and gazes at us through two large, blue glass marble eyes. She carries a seal hide book of laws and holds aloft a fur torch. Her cotton dress featuring heart prints, it has been suggested, may signify Paniyak's personal fondness for Miss Liberty. *25/5563*

Figure 100. The Yukon-Kuskokwim Delta of southwest Alaska has abundant beach grass that women use to make baskets and, as shown here, circular mats. Jennie Sims replicates a scene from Yup'ik life—a woman sits on the floor, her legs extended, and completes a coiled grass mat. A finished mat is placed at her side. "Real life" scenes such as this are a means of teaching outsiders about Yup'ik activities and identity, and of reminding Yup'ik children about their values and their history. *25/5630*

Figure 101. This tableau won the Governor Janklow Best of Show Award at the Northern Plains Tribal Arts Show in 2002. Emil Her Many Horses created it to honor Lakota Vietnam Veterans. The military dolls carry an American flag, a POW flag, and a rifle; they wear beaded moccasins. Two of the women carry bird-wing fans, and two are waving white handkerchiefs. Among Lakota women, if a family member was involved in the military or accomplished a notable deed, then the female relatives had a right to acknowledge this by waving their bare hands, or handkerchiefs or fans in the air. *26/604*

artist Emil Her Many Horses created a tableau entitled *Honoring Our Lakota Vietnam Veterans* that calls upon the old-style Plains miniature tipis and dolls for inspiration but which pays homage to the courage and dedication of Lakota warriors today. Her Many Horses points out that Lakota warriors traditionally painted battle or horse raid scenes on their tipis as a way of marking their accomplishments. The designs on this tipi (figure 101) include beaded military helicopters, American flags, stars, and an eagle.

As a new wrinkle on an old form, commercial doll makers such as Pleasant Company (makers of American Girl) and Mattel have moved far beyond the old tourist-souvenir, made-in-Japan plastic dolls dressed in fluff and feathers, and have worked hard at replicating Native traditional clothing—in the case of Mattel's Barbie, presenting her in a series of "Collector Edition" outfits ranging from the Northwest Coast to the Plains to ancient Mexico. Pleasant Company, which creates dolls and books representing particular places and specific historical periods, received numerous requests for a Native American doll. They created Kaya, a doll depicting a Nez Perce girl growing up in 1764. Their approach to Kaya was indicative of a new attitude to Native people. The company sought permission from the Nez Perce tribe to make a doll, and worked with a tribal advisory group to develop Kaya's clothing and accessories, which included a leather parfleche, a dyed cornhusk bag, and replications of traditional foods such as camas root and huckleberries. As an additional innovation, they provided Kaya with clothing a Nez Perce girl of today might wear, including a jingle dress and a fancy shawl outfit, a recognition that Native people live in the modern world and yet continue to acknowledge their cultural traditions and identity. To date, Kaya has been a very popular addition to the American Girls Collection.

The future of Native American dolls and doll makers seems to be a bright one, holding the potential for economic rewards, educational benefits, and strengthened cultural values. Not all dolls are made solely for purchase; some people continue to make dolls for

Figure 102. This traditional rag doll by Judi Jourdan depicts a little Oneida girl in her finery. *25/6991*

friends and family rather than for sale. Such people recognize that the creation of a doll can bring personal satisfaction that transcends monetary reward. Some dolls, at least, will continue to be made as they have in the past, for pleasure, for pride, and as an outlet for creativity.

LIST OF DOLLS

The dolls listed below are from the collections of the National Museum of the American Indian and are illustrated in this book. Each listing includes:

The object name, including culture
Provenience
Approximate date
Materials
National Museum of the American Indian catalogue number and measurements in centimeters. Collection information where available. *References to publications illustrating or discussing the doll.*

FROM THE PAST

GOLD INKA WOMAN (fig. 8)
Peru
Ca. A.D. 1500
Cast gold
5/4120, height 23 cm
Purchased in Panama City through
Dr. E. G. Dexter, October, 1916
Dockstader (1967), Pl. 166.
The Metropolitan Museum of Art
(1973), fig. 115

BAHÍA WHISTLE FIGURINE (fig. 9)
Los Esteros, Bahía de Manta, Manabí,
Ecuador
200 B.C.–A.D. 500
Pottery, paint
24/463, height 28 cm
Gift of Dr. and Mrs. Anton Notey;

purchased from Augusto Bayas
Dockstader (1973), fig. 183

ANCIENT INUIT MAN (fig. 10)
Cape York, Greenland
A.D. 1400-1500
Wood
18/2998, height 6.5 cm.
Collected by Junius Bird

POTTERY FIGURINE (fig. 11)
Big Bone Bank, Posey County,
Indiana
A.D. 700–1600
Pottery, traces of red slip
5/6396, height 5.8 cm
Gift of Harmon W. Hendricks; C. F.
Artes Collection

TLATILCO REDWARE FIGURE
(fig. 12)
Sanbartolo, Valley of Mexico, Mexico
1500–600 B.C.
Pottery
22/708, height 8.9 cm
Coe (1965), fig. 82

"PRETTY LADY" (fig. 13)
Querendaro, Michoacán, Mexico
500 B.C.–A.D. 100
Pottery, paint
23/8701, height 12.4 cm
Gift of Dr. and Mrs. Arthur M. Sackler

WOMAN (fig. 14)
Colima, Mexico
300 B.C.–A.D. 300
Pottery, paint

23/5505, height 17.8 cm
Purchased from Fred C. Peterson

PLAYA DE LOS MUERTOS
WOMAN (fig. 15)
Rio Ulua, Belize
Ca. 1000–800 B.C.
Pottery, traces of red paint
4/3872, height 12.7 cm
Dr. J. E. Austin Collection
Dockstader (1964), fig. 141

"CHINESCO" FIGURE (fig. 16)
Nayarit, Mexico
300 B.C.–A.D. 300
Pottery, paint
23/7665, height 17.5 cm
Gift of Dr. Arthur M. Sackler

OLMEC MAN (fig. 18)
Las Bocas, Mexico
1000–500 B.C.
Pottery, white slip, paint
23/5495, height 8.3 cm
Purchased from Fred C. Peterson
Weaver (1981), Pl. 2, fig. C

VALDIVIA CLAY FIGURINE
(fig. 19)
Valdivia, Guayas, Ecuador
Ca. 3200 B.C.
Pottery, traces of red paint
24/8401, height 9 cm
Gift of Mrs. Alice K. Bache; purchased from James Judge
Dockstader (1973), fig. 181

MARIONETTE (fig. 20)
Joachin, Vera Cruz, Mexico
A.D. 500
Pottery, paint, cord (not original)
23/735, height 29.3 cm
Gift of the Marion Eppley Fund; purchased from Frances Pratt
Dockstader (1964), fig. 72

MAYA WHISTLE FIGURINE
(fig. 21)
Jaina Island, Campeche, Mexico
A.D. 700–1200
Pottery, paint, traces of cinnabar
23/2274, height 23.5 cm
Exchange from Furman Gallery
Dockstader (1964), fig. 81

AZTEC WOMAN (fig. 22)
Huexolta, Mexico
A.D. 1500
Pottery
1/2238, height 16.5 cm
Collected by G. Bauer

MOCHE MOTHER AND CHILD
(fig. 23)
Chicama Valley, Peru
A.D. 800–1000
Pottery
15/7679, height 19 cm
Henry Vanden Berg Collection

CASAS GRANDES EFFIGY JAR
(fig. 24)
Chihuahua, Mexico
A.D. 1060–1340
Pottery, painted
11/9878, height 11.5 cm
Purchased from Edward Ledwidge
in 1975

CHANCAY POTTERY DOLL (fig. 25)
Chancay, Ancash, Peru
A.D. 1000–1500
Pottery, paint
24/9499, height 64.7 cm

FOR PLAYING

TETON LAKOTA WOMAN (fig. 1)
South Dakota
Late 19th century
Buckskin, cloth, leather, beads, por-

cupine quills, tin cones and pendants, embroidery floss, ribbon
13/7839, height 27.3 cm

19th CENTURY PLAINS CAMP
SIOUX TIPI (fig. 26)
19th century
Hide, wood, paint, dyed and
wrapped porcupine quills, tin cones,
feathers, horsehair, porcupine (?)
hair, sinew, silk floss, string
2/9535, height 76.2 cm
Joseph Keppler Collection

TETON LAKOTA TIPI MODEL
(fig. 26)
ca. 1890
Hide, wood, paint, porcupine quills,
beads
12/2242, height 41 cm
George H. Bingenheimer Collection

COMANCHE HORSE AND RIDER
(fig. 26)
20th century
Buckskin, paint, beads, yarn, human
(?) hair, wood, bone, sinew, pony
skin, hide, rabbit, glue, feathers
22/4820, height 24.2 cm
Gift of Dr. and Mrs. Otho C. Hudson
in memory of their daughter Mrs.
Dorothy Hudson Mavroyanis
Lavitt (1982), p. 100

SIOUX GIRL (fig. 26)
19th century
Buckskin, paint, buffalo-calf hair,
beads, sinew
8836, height 16 cm
Joseph Keppler Collection

COMANCHE CRADLEBOARD
(fig. 26)
Oklahoma
19th century
Wood, cloth, leather, beads, silk,
brass nails, human (?) hair, embroidery floss
2/1535, height 16.5 cm
Collected by M. R. Harrington

INUIT KAYAK WITH MAN (fig. 29)
East Coast of Greenland
19th century
Sealskin (?), wood, ivory, sinew

19/6279, length 51.8 cm
Purchased in London, England, by
George C. Heye

YUP'IK ESKIMO WOMAN (fig. 31)
Kuskokwim River, Alaska
Ca. 1905
Ivory, Arctic squirrel skin and claws,
caribou hair, cloth, metal, yarn
9/3626, height 17.7 cm
A. H. Twitchell Collection

INUIT WOMAN (fig. 32)
Ammassalik, Greenland
Late 19th–early 20th century
Wood, hide, fur, sinew
11/3078, height 14 cm
Exchange from Nationalmuseet,
Copenhagen, Denmark

CENTRAL POMO BABY IN
CARRIER (fig. 33)
Yokaia, California
Late 19th–early 20th century
Willow (?), twine, china doll, cloth,
clam shell beads, string
20/7144, height 12.7 cm
Exchange with Museum of Art,
Rhode Island School of Design

BLACKFEET WOMAN (fig. 34)
Montana
Ca.1850
Wood, trade cloth, ribbons, beads
23/4604, height 36.2 cm
Exchange with Schenectady Museum
Association
The Nelson R. Perry Collection;
collected near the Canadian border
in 1860
*Museum of the American Indian
(1965).*
Fox (1972), Pl. 146

SIOUX "PIECES" DOLLS (fig. 35)
South Dakota
Collected 1890–1904
Cloth, paint, lace, embroidery floss,
straight pin
23/8270 (two specimens),
height 8.9 cm
Gift of Mrs. Pal Keleman; collected
by Septima V. Koehler, St. Elizabeth's
School, Rosebud, South Dakota

CHEYENNE WOMAN WITH A
STONE HEAD (fig. 36)
Wyoming
Ca. 1875
Stone, wood, buckskin, horsehair,
paint, beads, metal
23/850, height 40 cm
Gift of Mr. and Mrs. William R. Mor-
gan in behalf of Justin Morgan King;
collected by Mr. Fowler, 1880–1885
*Museum of the American Indian
(1965), Pl. 1*
Fox (1972), fig. 151
*See also Feder (1971), fig. 86, for
similar carved club*

BABY IN KIOWA CRADLEBOARD
(fig. 37)
Anadarko, Oklahoma
Ca. 1890
Bisque head, wood, cloth, canvas,
hide, beads
23/6804, height 49.5 cm
Exchange from Joe F. Haines

MAHICAN/STOCKBRIDGE CORN-
HUSK DOLL (fig. 39)
Stockbridge, Wisconsin
Early 20th century
Cornhusk, trade cloth, buffalo hair,
beads, paint
16/5487, height 25.5 cm
Collected by Paul Warner
Lavitt (1982), p. 34

ANISHINAABE (OJIBWE) DOLL IN
CRADLEBOARD (fig. 40)
Collected from the Teton Lakota
Early 20th century
Wood, cloth, velvet, hide, beads,
nails, silk thread, embroidery floss,
ink (?)
12/2180, height 43.2 cm
George H. Bingenheimer Collection

OLD CREE WOMAN (fig. 41)
Canada
20th century
Wood, cloth, hide, caribou hair,
paint, yarn
24/1833, height 17.5 cm
Exchange with Jackson Hole
Preserve
The David C. Vernon Collection

CHIRICAHUA APACHE GIRL
(fig. 42)
Arizona
19th century
Wood, hide, paint, cloth, beads,
horsehair, sinew, tin, brass
16/1347, height 40.6 cm
Gift of Mrs. Alexander H. Richardson
and Mrs. Alexander W. Maish
Major John G. Bourke Collection

"STICK" DOLL (fig. 44)
Northern Mexico
Mid-20th century
Wood, cloth, paint, beads, yarn,
straight pins
22/8740, height 17 cm
Gift of Irving B. Levi

ZAPOTEC PAINTED WOODEN
DOLL (fig. 45)
Oaxaca, Mexico
20th century
Wood, paint
21/8807, height 22.2 cm

SERI CLOTH DOLL (fig. 46)
Baja California, Mexico
Ca. 1960
Cloth, thread
24/8437, height 12.7 cm
Collected by Richard A. White, Jr.,
1965–1970

QUICHE MAN (fig. 47)
Santiago Atitlan, Guatemala
Mid-20th century
China doll, cloth, embroidery floss
22/4791, height 28 cm
Gift of Dr. and Mrs. Otho C. Hudson
in memory of their daughter Mrs.
Dorothy Hudson Mavroyanis

KARAJA DOLLS (fig. 48)
Left:
KARAJA DOLL DEPICTING
WOMAN HOLDING BOWL
Santa Isabel, Brazil
Made by Shurerea
Ca. 1960
Pottery, bark, paint
23/1562, height 10.9 cm.
Collected by Borys Malkin in 1961

Center:
KARAJA DOLL DEPICTING
WOMAN HOLDING CHILD
Santa Isabel, Brazil
Made by Shurerea
Ca. 1960
Pottery, bark, paint
23/1562, height 13.6 cm.
Collected by Borys Malkin in 1961

Right:
KARAJA DOLL DEPICTING
YOUNG GIRL HOLDING DOLL
OR BABY
Santa Isabel, Brazil
Made by Shurerea
Ca. 1960
Pottery, bark, paint
23/1562, height 10.9 cm
Collected by Borys Malkin in 1961

SHIPIBO BALSA WOOD FIGURE
(fig. 49)
Rio Calleria, Ucayali, Peru
1961
Balsa wood, paint
23/1613, height 50.8 cm
Gift of Malcolm Delacorte; collected
by Borys Malkin, 1961

TAPIRAPÉ BEESWAX DOLL (fig. 50)
Mato Grosso, Brazil
Ca.1961
Cane (?), beeswax
23/1510, height 29.2 cm
Collected by Borys Malkin, 1961

WOODEN DOLL (fig. 51)
Rio Capayas, Esmeraldas, Ecuador
Ca. 1900
Wood
2/3594, height 29.2 cm
Collected by S. A. Barrett

QUECHUA COUPLE (fig. 52)
Peru
Ca. 1920
Yarn, silk floss, leather, sequins,
beads
10/7592, 10/7593, height
17.3 cm each
Fox (1972), Pl. 11

QUECHUA KNITTED DOLL (fig. 53)
Lima, Peru
Mid-20th century
Woolen yarn
23/9922, height 26.6 cm
Gift of Mr. Thomas Oblitas

FOR POWER

EKEKO DOLL (fig. 54 and 59)
Cusco, Peru
20th century
Pottery, gesso, paint, cloth, wood,
plastic, tobacco, paper, foodstuffs
21/8519, height 22 cm
Collected by Miss Beate R. Salz and
presented by the Wenner-Gren
Foundation in 1951

PRAIRIE POTAWATOMI DOLL
(fig. 56)
Kansas
Late 19th-early 20th century
Hide, horsehair, cloth, silk ribbon,
yarn, beads, animal claw, German-silver ornaments, wood, vermilion
24/1799, height 24.8 cm
Exchange with Jackson Hole Preserve, Inc.
The David C. Vernon Collection; collected from Bill Mexico
Lavitt (1982), p. 93

SHAWNEE EFFIGY DOLLS (fig. 58)
Oklahoma
Ca. 1900
woman Cloth, silk ribbon, hide,
metal, beads
2/1863, height 40 cm
Dr. W. C. Barnard Collection
man Cloth, hide, silk ribbon, beads
2/1871, height 51.5 cm
Collected by M.R. Harrington

SIOUX GHOST DANCERS (fig. 60)
Pine Ridge, South Dakota
Ca. 1900
man Hide, paint, beads, cloth, buffalo
hair, cowrie shell, eagle feathers,
sinew
9/7607, height 30.5 cm
Collected by Mrs. Emma Dow
*Museum of the American Indian
(1965)*

Fox (1972), Pl. 146
woman Hide, paint, beads, eagle
feathers, buffalo hair, porcupine
quills
9/7608, height 27.4 cm
Collected by Mrs. Emma Dow
Lavitt (1982), p. 101

INUPIAT ESKIMO MEDICINE
DOLL (fig. 61)
Diomede Island, Alaska
19th century
Wood, seal (?) gut, cloth, sinew,
ivory, beads, brass
5/9835, height 20.6 cm
Feder (1971), fig. 67

TANAINA MEDICINE DOLL (fig. 62)
Anchorage, Cook Inlet, Alaska
Early to mid-19th century
Wood, beads, cloth, hide, human
hair, ptarmigan feathers, baby caribou jawbone with teeth, yarn, dentalium shells, metal ornaments,
including military button, trade to-
kens, and brass cartridge shell casing
10/6091, height 26.8 cm
Gift of Mrs. Thea Heye

KUNA CURING DOLL (fig. 63)
Nargana Island, Panama
Late 19th-early 20th century
Wood, paint
11/4828, height 20 cm
Collected by D. E. Harrower

OTOMI PAPER DOLL (fig. 64)
San Pablito, Hidalgo, Mexico
20th century
Tissue paper
24/2920, height 26.6 cm
Gift of Dr. William M. Lannik

TAPIRAPÉ *TUPAN* FIGURE (fig. 65)
Brazil
20th century
Beeswax, feathers, down, string, shell
23/3997, height 40.6 cm
Purchased from Borys Malkin
Dockstader (1967), Pl. 220

FOR PERFORMANCE

WOODEN MARIONETTES
(fig. 66)
Nisga (on left)
British Columbia, Canada
19th century
Wood, paint, hide, graphite, string
8/2605, height 78 cm.
Collected by G. T. Emmons
Gitxsan (on right)
Kispiox, Upper Skeena River, British
Columbia
19th century
Wood, cloth, fur, hide, paint, puffin
beaks, metal, string
6/543, height 64 cm
Collected by G. T. Emmons

YUP'IK ESKIMO DANCE ORNA-
MENT (fig. 67)
Kuskokwim River, Alaska
Ca. 1905
Wood, paint, feather, hide
9/3578, length 30.5 cm
A. H. Twitchell Collection

YUP'IK ESKIMO DANCE ORNA-
MENT (fig. 68)
Kuskokwim River, Alaska
Ca. 1905
Wood, paint, feather, hide
9/3442, height 52.2 cm
Exchange with Julius Carlebach, July
1944; A. H. Twitchell Collection

INUPIAT ESKIMO EAGLE-WOLF
DANCERS (fig. 70)
Alaska
Ca. 1890
Wood, ivory, cloth, bladder (?) skin,
hide, paint, beads
6/9811 (two dolls), height 16.5 cm
D. F. Tozier Collection

DOLL SCULPTURE ENTITLED
SIEYUKTE (The Dance) (fig. 71)
Inupiaq Eskimo
Kobuk, Alaska
Made by Nita Hartman
1987
Ivory, soapstone, baleen, wood,
and furs (wolf, fox, muskrat, squirrel, and reindeer)
25/5234, height 21.5 cm; base
34.3 cm x 23.5 cm

Purchased from Alaska Heritage
Arts in Anchorage, Alaska
Indian Arts and Crafts Board Col-
lection, Department of the Interior,
at the National Museum of the
American Indian, Smithsonian
Institution

HOPI *TIHU,* KOYAALA (fig. 72)
Arizona
Ca. 1890
Cottonwood root (?), paint, denim,
cloth, velvet, cornhusk, string, nails
19/4087, height 30.5 cm
William M. Fitzhugh Collection

HOPI *TIHU,* KOKOSORI (fig. 73)
Oraibi, Arizona
Ca. 1890
Cottonwood root (?), paint, cloth,
feathers, dyed horsehair, string
9/994, height 22.8 cm
Purchased from Fred Harvey

HOPI *TIHU,* ANGWUSNASOM-
TAQA (CROW MOTHER) (fig. 74)
Oraibi, Arizona
Ca. 1890
Cottonwood root (?), paint, feathers,
string
9/968, height 28 cm
Purchased from Fred Harvey

HOPI *TIHU,* HU'KATSINA (fig. 75)
Oraibi, Arizona
Ca. 1890
Cottonwood root (?), paint, hide,
eagle feathers, dyed horsehair,
yucca (?), string
18/6169, height 25.7 cm
Exchange with John L. Nelson
Collected by H. R. Voth, 1898 for
Field Museum, No. 66278

SAN JUAN DANCERS (fig. 76)
New Mexico
1960
woman—Basket Dancer Cloth, embroidery floss, yarn, feathers, beads,
rhinestone and imitation-silver jewelry, hide, paint, basketry, wood,
nail polish (?)
22/9571, height 29.8 cm
Purchased from Sallie Lippincott
man—Deer Dancer Cloth, embroi-

dery floss, paint, hide, fur, beads,
imitation-silver bracelet, yarn, bells,
wood, feathers, plastic greenery,
loose cotton, nail polish (?)
22/9572, height 35.5 cm
Purchased from Sallie Lippincott

ANISHINAABE (OJIBWE) DANCER
(fig. 77)
Wisconsin
20th century
Hide, cloth, beads, horsehair (?),
sinew
22/4763, height 16.5 cm
Gift of Dr. and Mrs. Otho C. Hudson
in memory of their daughter Mrs.
Dorothy Hudson Mavroyanis

WOMAN DANCER DOLLS
(fig. 78)
Oglala Lakota
Pine Ridge Reservation, South
Dakota
Made by Cecelia Fire Thunder
(Tawachin Waste Win)
Ca. 1990
dancer on left Hide, feathers, cloth,
glass and metal beads, shells, pigment, yarn
25/4702, height 40 cm
dancer on right Hide, feathers,
cloth, glass and metal beads, shells,
pigment, yarn, porcupine quills,
silk ribbon, metal tacks
25/4703, height 39 cm
Collected by and gift of Priscilla
(Pam) M. King, 1998

AYMARA FESTIVAL DANCER
(fig. 79) *on right*
Oruro, Bolivia
20th century
Cloth, velvet, leather, sequins, beads,
thread, wool
13/4497, height 35 cm
Collected by A. H. Verrill

AYMARA FESTIVAL DANCER
(fig. 79) *on left*
Oruro, Bolivia
20th century
Cloth, felt, yarn, leather, hair
13/4496, height 37.5 cm
Collected by A. H. Verrill

FOR PURCHASE

SEATED MALE DOLL (fig. 5)
Cup'ik Eskimo
Chevak, Alaska
Made by Anna Martins
Ca. 1975
Animal intestine and hide, fur,
plaid cotton cloth
25/5741, height 15 cm.
Indian Arts and Crafts Board Col-
lection, Department of the Interior,
at the National Museum of the
American Indian, Smithsonian
Institution

TWO NAVAJO DOLLS (fig. 80)
Sheep Springs, New Mexico
Made by Kay Bennett
Ca. 1965
Felt, cloth, yarn, sequins
woman on left 25/6988,
height 55.5 cm
woman on right 25/6989,
height 43 cm
Indian Arts and Crafts Board Col-
lection, Department of the Interior,
at the National Museum of the
American Indian, Smithsonian
Institution

"FLOR" DOLL (fig. 81)
Guanajuato, Mexico
1980
Papier-mâché, paint, yarn, silver glit-
ter
25/2194, height 23 cm
Gift of Mary Jane Lenz; collected by
Brenda S. Holland in Tijuana, Mexico

QUECHUA MAN (fig. 82)
Peru
Ca. 1935
Cloth, pottery, paint, hide, buttons,
rickrack, gold tinsel, string
22/4808, height 29.3 cm
Gift of Dr. and Mrs. Otho C. Hudson
in memory of their daughter Mrs.
Dorothy Hudson Mavroyanis

QUECHUA WOMAN (fig. 82)
Peru
Ca. 1935
Pottery, paint, cloth, rickrack, but-
tons, leather, metal, cardboard, tooth-
pick, yarn

22/4809, height 28.2 cm
Gift of Dr. and Mrs. Otho C. Hudson
in memory of their daughter Mrs.
Dorothy Hudson Mavroyanis

WOMAN WITH BROOM (fig. 83)
Guatemala
20th century
Cloth, metal beads, wood, straw
22/3685, height 18.5 cm
Gift of Mrs. G. C. Fritts

MAPUCHE MAN ON HORSE
(fig. 84)
Central Chile
Ca. 1925
Pottery, horsehide, feathers, cloth,
yarn, metal, woolen blankets, hide,
beads, chrome studs, sinew, twine,
leather
17/6662, height 26 cm
Gift of Mrs. Thea Heye; purchased in
Hamburg, Germany, by George G.
Heye
Fox (1972), Pl. 163

ANISHINAABE (OJIBWE)
HIAWATHA, MINNEHAHA,
AND NOKOMIS (fig. 85)
Upper Great Lakes
Ca. 1940
man (Hiawatha) Pottery, paint, cut-
up kid gloves, velvet, ermine tails,
feathers, beads, silk floss, commercial
doll's hair, wood
22/4760, height 35 cm
woman on right (Minnehaha) Pottery,
paint, cut-up kid gloves, cloth, silk
floss, feathers, beads, plastic bear
claw, brass, commercial doll's hair
22/4761, height 29.8 cm
woman on left (Nokomis)
Pottery, paint, suede, beads, commercial doll's hair
22/4762, height 35.5 cm
Gift of Dr. and Mrs. Otho C. Hudson
in memory of their daughter Mrs.
Dorothy Hudson Mavroyanis

ALEUT *BAIDARKA* (fig. 86)
Collected in the Kuskokwim region
of Alaska
Ca. 1880
Wood, seal (?) bladder skin, paint,
beads, seal (?) whiskers, sinew, yarn

16/8275, length 49.9 cm
Gift of Dr. and Mrs. A. Eugene Austin

HURON COUPLE (fig. 87)
Lorette, Quebec, Canada
Early 20th century
Wood, paint, cloth, yarn, leather
man 20/5053, height 28 cm
woman 20/5054, height 26.7 cm
Collected by F. G. Speck
Museum of the American Indian
(1965)

SEMINOLE MAN (fig. 88)
Big Cypress Reservation, Hendry
County, Florida
Ca. 1935
Palmetto fiber, embroidery floss,
cloth, beads
22/1549, height 37.5 cm
Collected and presented by Mrs.
Ethel Cutler Freeman

CHEROKEE MOTHER AND CHILD
(fig. 89)
Qualla Reservation, North Carolina
Ca. 1940
Wood, paint, cloth, embroidery floss
20/9729, height 20.3 cm

YUMA AND MOHAVE CLAY
DOLLS (fig. 90)
Arizona
Late 19th-early 20th century
Yuma Pottery, cloth, embroidery floss,
beads, horsehair, string
18/9720, height 18.5 cm
Mrs. M. Alta Richards Collection
Mohave Pottery, paint, cloth, beads,
horsehair
19/4106, height 22 cm
William M. Fitzhugh Collection

PUEBLO DOLLS (fig. 91)
New Mexico
Ca. 1890
Pottery, paint
Cochiti man (on left) 6/6821, height
23 cm
Elihu B. Taft Collection
Santo Domingo man (on right)
15/3508, height 22 cm
Presented by Mrs. Alice de Santiago

STORYTELLER DOLL WITH 10
CHILDREN (fig. 92)
Cochiti, New Mexico
Made by Helen Cordero
Ca. 1969
Clay, paint
25/9180, height 27 cm
Purchased for Indian Arts and
Crafts Board in 1970
Transferred from the Department
of the Interior/Indian Arts and
Crafts Board Headquarters
Collection

TOHONO O'ODHAM BASKETRY
DOLL (fig. 93)
Arizona
Made by Gloria Ramon of Santa Rosa
for the Pima County Livestock Show
1960
White and green yucca, black devil's
claw (*martynia*)
22/9077, height 35.5 cm
Gift of Mr. Tom Bahti

KATSINA DOLL CALLED DAWA
(Sun katsina) (fig. 94)
Hopi Pueblo
Arizona
Made by Story Huma
Ca. 1968
Cottonwood, paint, feathers, rick-
rack trim
25/5576, height 37.5 cm
Purchase from Hopi Silver Craft
and Arts & Craft Guild in 1968
Indian Arts and Crafts Board Col-
lection, Department of the Interior,
at the National Museum of the
American Indian, Smithsonian
Institution

DOLL REPRESENTING
KOSHARE (Hano clown) (fig. 95)
Hopi
Arizona
Made by Cal Yestewa
Ca. 1982
Cottonwood, paint, beads, cloth,
cornhusk
25/5588, height 27.5 cm
Purchased from Department of the
Interior Craft Shop in 1982
Indian Arts and Crafts Board Col-
lection, Department of the Interior,

at the National Museum of the
American Indian, Smithsonian
Institution

BERRY PICKER AND HUNTER
DOLLS, a pair (fig. 96)
Inupiat Eskimo
Kotzebue, Alaska
Made by Ethel Washington
(1889–1967)
1964
Birch wood, ground squirrel and cari-
bou skins, cloth, birchbark, bone
woman 25/5301, height 26.5 cm
man 25/5302, height 30.5 cm
Indian Arts and Crafts Board Col-
lection, Department of the Interior,
at the National Museum of the
American Indian, Smithsonian
Institution

ONEIDA HUNTER (fig. 97)
Red Hook, New York
Made by Steven Chrisjohn
Ca. 1982
Wrapped cornhusk, leather, beads,
artificial hair, feathers, flint, ivory,
silver, copper, sinew
25/9271, height 30.3 cm
Purchased from DOI Indian
Craft Shop
Transferred from the Department
of the Interior/Indian Arts and
Crafts Board Headquarters
Collection

DOLL IN A BIKINI (fig. 98)
Oneida Iroquois
Wisconsin
Made by Judi Jourdan
Ca. 1980
Stuffed nylon, yarn, cotton, satin,
silver chain
25/5778, length 37 cm
Indian Arts and Crafts Board Col-
lection, Department of the Interior,
at the National Museum of the
American Indian, Smithsonian
Institution

DOLL SCULPTURE MY LOVE,
MISS LIBERTY (fig. 99)
Cup'ik Eskimo
Chevak, Alaska
Made by Rosalie Paniyak
1987
Sea lion intestine overdress,
printed fabric underdress, fur,
seal hide, wood, blue glass marbles
25/5563, height 84 cm
Indian Arts and Crafts Board Col-
lection, Department of the Interior,
at the National Museum of the
American Indian, Smithsonian
Institution

MAT MAKER DOLL (fig. 100)
Yup'ik Eskimo
Toksook Bay, Alaska
Made by Jennie Sims
Ca. 1982
Driftwood, loonskin, muskrat and
rabbit fur, suede, imitation fur
25/5630, height 22.9 cm
Purchased from Yugtarvic Regional
Museum in 1982
Indian Arts and Crafts Board Col-
lection, Department of the Interior,
at the National Museum of the
American Indian, Smithsonian
Institution

HONORING OUR LAKOTA
VIETNAM VETERANS (fig. 101)
Oglala Lakota, Pine Ridge,
South Dakota
Made by Emil Her Many Horses
2002
Deer hide, brass and glass beads,
wool cloth, feathers, dentalium
shells, plastic miniature elk teeth,
American flag, wood
26/604, height of tipi 80.5 cm
Tallest woman 30 cm
Tallest man 29.5 cm
Museum purchase

RAG DOLL (fig. 102)
Oneida Iroquois
Wisconsin
Made by Judi Jourdan
Ca. 1980
Fabric, lace, ribbon, suede, yarn,
wood, glass, brass metal, plastic, shell
25/6991, height 71 cm
Indian Arts and Crafts Board Col-
lection, Department of the Interior,
at the National Museum of the
American Indian, Smithsonian
Institution

NOTES

FROM THE PAST

1. Ekholm, p. 175.
2. Tuck.
3. See figure 6, p. 364, *Handbook of North American Indians*, vol. 5, 1984, Smithsonian Institution.
4. Mathews.
5. Willoughby, pp. 71–74.
6. This drawing has been frequently reproduced. One recent source is Hulton, fig, 26, p. 128.
7. Morss, p. 61.
8. Haury, cited in Dockstader, 1985, p. 100.
9. Roosevelt.
10. Barbour, p. 25.
11. Reichel-Dolmatoff, pp. 236–238. He appears not to have questioned any women with this topic. Morss, however, reports that in the 1920s at an archaeological site in the American Southwest, a Pueblo workman's wife actually used one of the small newly excavated figures to relieve the pains of childbirth and secure a successful delivery. The piece was apparently worn as an amulet.
12. Meggers and Evans, p. 100.
13. Lathrap, p. 39.
14. de Borhegyi, p. 274.
15. Ekholm, p. 186.
16. Pasztory, et al., exhibit #5.
17. Lilien.
18. *National Geographic*, vol. 144, no. 6, December 1973, p. 733.

FOR PLAYING

1. Fraser, p. 7. See also Fox, p. 355, note 15.
2. White.
3. Theodore De Bry, *America* (Frankfurt, Germany: 1590). Reproduced in Hulton, p. 114, fig. 12.
4. Gillham, cited in Fair, p. 51.
5. Ray, 1981, p. 22.
6. Nelson, p. 345.
7. Fair, p. 55.
8. Nelson, pp. 497–99.
9. James G. Swan. *The Northwest Coast*. New York: Harper and Brothers, 1857, cited in Lavitt, p. 109.
10. Hilger, 1952, p. 107.
11. Linderman, p. 25.
12. Kant, p. 37.
13. Dorsey, p. 329.
14. Linderman, p. 29.
15. Jeffrey Brain, personal communication.
16. Opler, p. 40.
17. Rain Parrish, personal communication.
18. Lang and Walters, p. 58. (In Kelly, Lang, and Walters).
19. McGee, p. 290.

FOR POWER

1. Eliade, p. 4.
2. Antoine Denis Raudot, cited in Kinietz, pp. 372–374.
3. P. Jones, *History of the Ojibway Indians*, London, n.d., p. 146, cited in Frazer, p. 7.
4. Harrington, 1921, pp. 162–163.
5. Harrington, *ibid.* p. 162.
6. Harrington, *ibid.* p. 170.
7. Harrington, unpublished field notes in the archives of the National Museum of the American Indian.
8. Densmore, 1918, pp. 77ff. See also Densmore 1948, p. 186 and plate XVIf.
9. Skinner, 1925, vol. II, p. 71.
10. Skinner, 1925, p. 69.
11. Howard, 1955, p. 172.
12. W. H. Keating. *Narrative of an Expedition to the Source of St. Peter's River*. London, 1825 ii 159, cited in Frazer, p. 11.
13. Wildschut, 1975, p. 123.
14. Wildschut, 1926, p. 102.
15. Birket-Smith and De Laguna, p. 502.
16. Erman, 1870–71, *Ethnographische Wahrnehmungen und Erfahrungen an den Kusten des Berings-Meeres*, ZE II-III, cited in Birket-Smith and De Laguna, p. 502.
17. Alan Stahl, American Numismatic Society, personal communication.
18. David Ebersole, personal communication.
19. Dan Wharton, Bronx Zoo, personal communication.
20. Stout, p. 266.
21. Sandstrom, p. 68.

FOR PERFORMANCE

1. Dunn, p. 250.
2. Dunn, pp. 248–249.
3. Suzanne Bernardi, cited in Ray, 1977, p. 16.
4. Knud Rasmussen, cited in Ray, 1977, p. 16.
5. Jose Montaño, personal communication.

FOR PURCHASE

1. *Doll Talk*, vol. 17, no. 9, Nov.-Dec. 1968, p. 16.
2. *Doll Talk*, vol. 14, no. 9, Nov.-Dec. 1962, p. 5.
3. *Doll Talk*, vol. 16, no. 6, May-June 1966, pp. 2–3.
4. *Doll Talk*, vol. 20, no. 12, May-June 1975, p. 11.
5. *Doll Talk*, vol. 20, no. 11, March-April 1975, pp. 4–5.
6. *Doll Talk*, vol. 5, no. 1, Oct.-Dec. 1944, p. 4.
7. *Doll Talk*, vol. 15, no. 4, Jan.-Feb. 1964, p. 3.
8. *Doll Talk*, vol. 15, no. 9, Nov.-Dec. 1964, p. 7.
9. Henry B. Collins in Fitzhugh and Kaplan, p. 29. Also see Nelson, p. 373.
10. Ray, 1981, p. 60.
11. These dolls are illustrated on the cover of *American Indian Art*, vol. 10, no. 1, Winter 1984.
12. Cited in King, p. 90.
13. Gordon, p. 279.
14. Downs, pp. 49–50.
15. West, p. 61.
16. *Doll Talk*, vol. 19, no. 12, May-June 1973, pp. 1–3.
17. Barbara Babcock, personal communication.
18. Holmes.
19. Babcock, p. 31.
20. Cited in *Southwest Art*, August 2001, p. 239.
21. See Lee, 1999 for a useful overview of Alaskan doll makers.

PHOTO CREDITS

BIBLIOGRAPHY

ABBREVIATIONS:

AA   American Anthropologist

AIA   American Indian Art Magazine

AMNH   American Museum of Natural History, New York

BAE/AR   Bureau of American Ethnology Annual Report, Washington, D.C.

BAE/B   Bureau of American Ethnology Bulletin, Washington, D.C.

HMAI   Handbook of Middle American Indians, ed. Robert Wauchope, Austin: University of Texas Press, 1965–84.

HNAI   Handbook of North American Indians, ed. William C. Sturtevant, Washington, D.C.: Smithsonian Institution

MAI-HF   Museum of the American Indian, Heye Foundation, New York

Abel-Vidor, Suzanne, Ronald L. Bishop, Warwick Bray, Elizabeth Kennedy Easby, Oscar Fonesca Zamora, Hector Gamboa Paniagua, Luis Diego Gomez Pignataro, Mark M. Graham, Frederick W. Lange, Michael J. Snarskis, Lambertus van Zelst. *Between Continents/Between Seas: Pre-Columbian Art of Costa Rica*. New York: Harry N. Abrams, Inc., in association with the Detroit Institute of Arts. 1981.

Adams, Richard E. W. *Prehistoric Mesoamerica*. Boston: Little, Brown and Company. 1977.

Anonymous. *Indian Dolls*. New York: MAI-HF. 1965.

Babcock, Barbara A. *Clay Changes: Helen Cordero and the Pueblo Storyteller. AIA* vol. 8, no. 2, pp. 30–39. 1983.

Babcock, Barbara A. and Guy and Doris Monthan. *The Pueblo Storyteller: Development of a Figurative Ceramic Tradition*. Tucson: University of Arizona Press. 1986.

Barbour, Warren. "The Figurines and Figurine Chronology of Ancient Teotihuacan, Mexico." Ph.D. dissertation, University of Rochester, New York. 1976.

Batkin, Jonathan. "Tourism is Overrated: Pueblo Pottery and the Early Curio Trade, 1880–1910." In *Unpacking Culture: Art and Commodity in Colonial and Postcolonial Worlds*. Eds. Ruth B. Phillips and Christopher B. Steiner. Pp. 159–189. Berkeley: University of California Press. 1999.

Bell, Betty. "Archaeology of the Nayarit, Jalisco, and Colima." *HMAI* vol. 11, part 2, pp. 694–753. 1965.

Bennett, Kay. *Kaibah: Recollections of a Navajo Girlhood*. Los Angeles: Western Lore Press. 1964.

Birket-Smith, Kaj and Frederick De Laguna. *The Eyak Indians of the Copper River Delta, Alaska. Det. Kgl. Danske Videnskabernes Selskab*. Copenhagen: Levin and Munksgaard. 1938.

Boas, Franz. "The Social Organization and the Secret Societies of the Kwakiutl Indians." *Report of the United States National Museum*. Washington, D.C. 1895.

von Boehn, Max. *Dolls and Puppets*. Trans. Josephine Nicoll. Newton Centre, Mass.: Charles T. Branford. 1956 rev. ed. Originally published as *Puppen und Puppenspiele*. Munchen: F. Bruckmann. 1929.

Bonar, Eulalie H. *Woven by the Grandmothers: Nineteenth-Century Navajo Textiles from the National Museum of the American Indian*. Washington, DC: Smithsonian Institution Press. 1996.

Borhegyi, Stephan de. "Jointed Figurines in Mesoamerica and Their Cultural Implication." *Southwestern Journal of Anthropology* 10 (3): pp. 268–277, 1954.

Brawer, Catherine Coleman, editor. *Many Trails: Indians of the Lower Hudson Valley*. Katonah, N.Y.: The Katonah Gallery. 1983.

Breunig, Robert and Michael Lomatuway'ma. "Kachina Dolls." *Plateau*. vol. 54, no. 4. Flagstaff: Museum of Northern Arizona. 1983.

Burland, Cottie. *North American Indian Mythology*. London: The Hamlyn Publishing Group Ltd. 1965.

Butler, M. "A Study of Maya Mold-made Figurines." *AA* n.s. 37: pp. 636–673. 1953.

Callender, Charles. "Miami." *HNAI*, vol. 5, pp. 681–689. 1978.

Chan, Roman Pina. "Preclassic or Formative Pottery and Minor Arts of the Valley of Mexico." *HMAI* vol. 10, part 1, pp. 157–178. 1965.

Cleland, Charles F. "Yuma Dolls." *AIA* vol. 5, no. 3, pp. 36–41. 1980.

Coe, Michael D. *The Jaguar's Children: Preclassic Central Mexico*. New York: Museum of Primitive Art. 1965.

Collins, Henry B., Jr. "Archaeology of St. Lawrence Island, Alaska." *Smithsonian Miscellaneous Collections*, vol. 96, no. 1. Washington, D.C. 1937.

_____. "The Okvik Figure: Madonna or Bear Mother?" In *Native North American Art History: Selected Readings*. Eds. Z. Mathews and A. Jonaitis. Palo Alto: Peek Publications. 1982. Originally published In *Folk, Dansk Ethnografisk Tidsskrift*. 11–12: pp. 125–132. 1969/70.

_____. "Additional Examples of Early Eskimo Art." In *Native North American Art History: Selected Readings*. Eds. Z. Mathews and A. Jonaitis. Palo Alto: Peek Publications. 1982. Originally published In *Folk, Dansk Ethnografisk Tidsskrift*. 16–17: pp. 55–62. 1974/75.

Colton, Harold S. *Hopi Kachina Dolls*. Albuquerque: University of New Mexico Press. 1949.

Cook de Leonard, Carmen. "Ceramics of the Classic Period in Central Mexico." *HMAI* vol. 10, part 1, pp. 1965.

Covarrubias, Miguel. *Mexico South: The Isthmus of Tehuantepec*. New York: Alfred A. Knopf. A Borzoi Book. 1946.

_____. *Indian Art of Mexico and Central America*. New York: Alfred A. Knopf. A Borzoi Book. 1966

Densmore, Frances. "Teton Sioux Music." *BAE/B* 61. Smithsonian Institution. 1918.

_____. "Chippewa Customs." *BAE/B* 86. Smithsonian Institution. 1929.

_____. "A Collection of Specimens from the Teton Sioux." *Indian Notes*. New York: MAI-HF. 1948.

Dockstader, Frederick J. "A Figurine Cache from Kino Bay, Sonora." In *Essays in Pre-Columbian Art and Archaeology*. Ed. Samuel K. Lothrop. Pp. 182–191. Cambridge: Harvard University Press. 1961.

_____. *Indian Art in America*. Greenwich: New York Graphic Society. 1961.

_____. *Indian Art in Middle America*. Greenwich: New York Graphic Society. 1964.

_____. *Indian Art in South America*. Greenwich: New York Graphic Society. 1967.

_____. *Indian Art in the Americas*. New York: MAI/HF. 1973.

_____. *Masterworks from the Museum of the American Indian*. New York: Metropolitan Museum of Art. 1973.

_____. *The Kachina and the White Man*. Albuquerque: University of New Mexico Press. 1985. Originally published as *Bulletin 35 of the Cranbrook Institute of Science*. Bloomfield Hills, Michigan. 1954.

Doll Talk—A magazine in miniature published for doll enthusiasts. "Issued about every eight weeks." Published by Kimport Dolls, Independence, Missouri.

Dorsey, J. Owen. "Games of Teton Dakota Children." *AA* (4) pp. 329–346. 1891.

Downs, Dorothy. "British Influences on Creek and Seminole Men's Clothing 1733–1858." *The Florida Anthropologist*, vol. 33, no. 2, pp. 46–65. Coral Gables: University of Miami. 1980.

Driver, Harold E. *Indians of North America*. Chicago: The University of Chicago Press. 1969.

Drucker, Philip. *Indians of the Northwest Coast*. New York: McGraw-Hill Book Company. 1955. Reprinted for the American Museum of Natural History as an American Museum Science Books edition, 1963.

Dunn, J. H. "Puppets of the Skeena." *Canadian Geographical Journal*, no. 47, pp. 248–252. 1953.

Ekholm, Susanna M. "The Lagartero Figurines." In *Maya Archaeology and Ethnohistory*. Eds. N. Hammond and J. G. Willey. Pp. 172–186. Austin: University of Texas Press. 1979.

Eliade, Mircea. *Shamanism: Archaic Techniques of Ecstasy*. Bollingen Series LXXVI. Trans. Willard L. Trask. Princeton: Princeton University Press. 1964. Originally published in French as *Le Chamanisme et les techniques archaiques d'extase* by Librairie Payot, Paris, 1951.

Ewers, John C. *The Horse in Blackfoot Culture*. *BAE/B* 159. Smithsonian. 1955. Reprinted as Classics of Smithsonian Anthropology Edition, 1980.

Fair, Susan W. *Eskimo Dolls*. Exhibit catalog published by the Alaska State Council on the Arts, Anchorage. Ed. Suzi Jones. 1982.

Fawcett, David M. "The Featherworker: The Karaja of Brazil." In *The Ancestors: Native Artisans of the Americas*. Eds. Anna C. Roosevelt and James G. E. Smith. New York: MAI. 1979.

Feder, Norman. *Two Hundred Years of North American Indian Art*. New York: Praeger Publishers. 1971.

Fitzhugh, William W. and Susan A. Kaplan. *Inua: Spirit World of the Bering Sea Eskimo*. Washington, D.C.: Smithsonian Institution Press. 1982.

Fox, Carl. *The Doll*. New York: Harry N. Abrams. 1973.

Fraser, Antonia. *Dolls*. London: Weidenfeld and Nicolson. 1963.

Frazer, Sir James G. *The New Golden Bough* (abridged). Ed. Theodore H. Gaster. New York: Criterion Books. 1959. First published in England in 1890 in a two-volume edition, later expanded to 12 volumes and a supplement.

Furst, Peter T. *The Ninth Level: Funerary Art from Ancient Mesoamerica*. Iowa City: The University of Iowa Museum of Art. 1978.

Gebhart-Sayer, Angelika. *The Cosmos Encoiled: Indian Art of the Peruvian Amazon*. New York: Center for Inter-American Relations. 1984.

Gérin, Léon. "The Hurons of Lorette." *Report of the British Association for the Advancement of Science*. vol. 70, pp. 549–568. 1900.

Gillham, Charles E. *Medicine Men of Hooper Bay*. New York: MacMillan Company. 1955.

Gordon, Beverly. "The Niagara Falls Whimsey: The Object as a Symbol of Cultural Interface." Ph.D. Dissertation, University of Wisconsin. 1984.

Gow-Smith, Francis. "The Arawana, or Fish Dance, of the Caraja Indians of Matto Grosso, Brazil." In *Indian Notes*, vol. 2, no. 2, pp. 96–99. New York: MAI-HF. 1925.

Graburn, Nelson H. H., editor. *Ethnic and Tourist Arts: Cultural Expressions from the Fourth World*. Berkeley: University of California Press. 1976.

Grinnell, George Bird. *The Cheyenne Indians*. New Haven: Yale University Press. 1923.

Harrington, Mark R. *Religion and Ceremonies of the Lenape. Indian Notes and Monographs. Miscellaneous Series*, no. 19. New York: MAI-HF. 1921.

_____. "Sacred Bundles of the Sac and Fox." *Anthropological Publications of the University of Pennsylvania*, vol. IV, no. 2. 1924.

Hartmann, Günther. *Litjoko: Puppen der Karaja, Brasilien*. Berlin: Museum für Volkerkunde. 1973.

Hedrick, Basil C. and Susan Pickel-Hedrick. *Ethel Washington: The Life and Times of an Eskimo Doll Maker. Alaska Historical Commission Studies in History*, no. 31. 1983.

Hilger, M. Inez. *Chippewa Child Life and Its Cultural Background. BAE/B* 146. Smithsonian Institution. 1951.

_____. *Arapaho Child Life and Its Cultural Background. BAE/B* 148. 1952.

Hoffman, William J. *The Midewiwin or Grand Medicine Society of the Ojibwa. BAE/AR* no. 7. Smithsonian Institution. 1891.

Holmes, William H. "The Debasement of Pueblo Art." *AA* (o.s.), 2: 230. 1889.

Howard, James H. "The Tree Dweller Cults of the Dakota." *Journal of American Folklore*, vol. 68, pp. 169-1955.

Howard, James H. and Marshall Gettys. "The Harkins Choctaw Dolls as a Source of Choctaw Culture History." *Bulletin of Oklahoma Anthropological Society*, vol. 32. 1983.

Hulton, Paul. *America 1585: The Complete Drawings of John White*. University of North Carolina Press and British Museum Publications. 1984.

Hungry Wolf, Adolf and Beverly. *Blackfoot Craftworker's Book. Good Medicine Series*, no. 15. Invermere, British Columbia. 1977.

Hungry Wolf, Beverly. *The Ways of My Grandmothers*. New York: William Morrow. 1980.

Josephy, Jr., Alvin M. *The Indian Heritage of America*. New York: Alfred A. Knopf. 1969.

Kant, Juanita. *Old Style Plains Dolls. The South Dakota Museum*, vol. II, no. 1. Vermilion, S.D.: University of South Dakota. 1975.

Kelly, Roger E., R. W. Lang, and Harry Walters. *Navaho Figurines Called Dolls*. Santa Fe: Museum of Navaho Ceremonial Arts, Inc. 1972.

Kidder, A.V. and E. M. Shook. "A Possibly Unique Type of Formative Figurine from Guatemala." In *Essays in Pre-Columbian Art and Archaeology*. Ed. Samuel K. Lothrop. Cambridge: Harvard University Press. 1961.

King, J. C. H. *Thunderbird and Lightning: Indian Life in Northeastern North America 1600–1900*. London: British Museum Publications Ltd. 1982.

Kinietz, W. Vernon. *The Indians of the Western Great Lakes: 1615–1760*. Ann Arbor: The University of Michigan Press. 1965. First published by the University of Michigan Press, 1940.

Kroeber, A. L. *Handbook of the Indians of California. BAE/B* 78. Smithsonian Institution. 1925. Republished as a paperback edition by Dover Publications, Inc., New York, 1976.

LaBarre, Weston. "The Aymara Indians of the Lake Titicaca Plateau, Bolivia." *Memoir* 68, *AA* vol. 50, no. 1, part 2. 1948.

Landes, Ruth. *The Prairie Potawatomi: Tradition and Ritual in the Twentieth Century*. Madison: The University of Wisconsin Press. 1970.

Lannik, W., R. L. Palm, and M. P. Tatkon. *Paper Figures and Folk Medicine Among the San Pablito Otomi. Indian Notes and Monographs, Miscellaneous Series*, no. 57. New

York: MAI-HF. 1969.

Lathrap, Donald W. *Ancient Ecuador: Culture, Clay and Creativity 3000–300 B. C.* Chicago: Field Museum of Natural History. 1975.

Lavitt, Wendy. *American Folk Dolls.* New York: Alfred A. Knopf, Inc. 1982.

Lee, Molly C. editor. *Not Just a Pretty Face: Dolls and Human Figurines in Alaska Native Cultures.* Fairbanks: University of Alaska Museum. 1999.

Lee, Jr., Thomas A. "The Artifacts of Chiapa de Corzo, Chiapas, Mexico." *Papers of the New World Archaeological Foundation*, no. 26. Provo, Utah: Brigham Young University. 1969.

Lévi-Strauss, Claude. *The Savage Mind.* Chicago: The University of Chicago Press. 1966. Originally published as *La Pensee Sauvage*, Librairie Plon, Paris, 1962.

Libhart, Myles. "To Dress with Great Care: Contemporary American Indian and Eskimo Doll Artists of the United States." *American Indian Art.* vol. 14, no. 2, p. 47. Spring 1989.

Lilien (Solecki), R. M. "A Study of Central Andean Ceramic Figurines." Ph.D. dissertation, Columbia University, 1956.

Linderman, Frank B. *Blackfeet Indians.* St. Paul, Minnesota: The Great Northern Railway. 1935.

_____. *Pretty-Shield: Medicine Woman of the Crows.* Lincoln: University of Nebraska Press. Originally published as *Red Mother*, 1932.

Lowie, Robert H. *Indians of the Plains.* New York: McGraw-Hill. 1954.

Lyford, Carrie A. *Iroquois Crafts.* Stevens Point, Wisconsin: Schneider Publishers. 1982. Originally printed as part of the *Indian Handcraft Series* published by the Bureau of Indian Affairs.

Maccauley, Clay. *The Seminole Indians*

of Florida. BAE/AR no. 5. 1883.

McGee, W. J. *The Seri Indians. BAE/AR* no. 17, part 1. 1898. Reprinted as *A Rio Grande Classic* by The Rio Grande Press, Inc., Glorieta, N.M., 1971.

McIlwraith, T. F. *The Bella Coola Indians.* 2 vols. Toronto: University of Toronto Press. 1948.

Mathews, Zena P. and Aldona Jonaitis, editors. *Native North American Art History: Selected Readings.* Palo Alto: Peek Publications. 1982.

Mathews, Zena P. "Seneca Figurines: A Case of Misplaced Modesty." In Mathews and Jonaitis, 1982, pp. 293–310.

Maxwell, James A., editor. *America's Fascinating Indian Heritage.* Pleasantville, N.Y.: The Reader's Digest Association, Inc. 1978.

Meggers, Betty J. and Clifford Evans. "A Transpacific Contact in 3000 B.C." First published in *Scientific American*, January, 1966. Republished in Zubrow, Fritz, and Fritz, pp. 97–104.

Miller, Mary Ellen. *The Art of Mesoamerica from Olmec to Aztec.* London and New York: Thames and Hudson, Inc. World of Art Series. 1986.

Moore, Lorene. "Dolls of the North American Indians." *Lore*, Winter, 1964.

Morss, Noel. "Cradled Infant Figurines from Tennessee and Mexico." *American Antiquity* 18 pp. 164–166. 1952.

_____. "Clay Figurines of the American Southwest." *Papers of the Peabody Museum of American Archaeology and Ethnology, Harvard University*, vol. XLIX, no. 1. Cambridge: Harvard University. 1954.

Muser, Curt. *Facts and Artifacts of Ancient Middle America.* New York: E. P. Dutton. 1978.

Nelson, Edward W. *The Eskimos About Bering Strait. BAE/AR* no. 18, part 1. 1899.

Opler, Morris E. *Childhood and Youth in Jicarilla Apache Society.* Los Angeles: Southwest Museum. 1946.

Osborn, Lilly de Jongh. *Indian Crafts of Guatemala and El Salvador.* Norman: University of Oklahoma Press. 1965.

Osborn, Lilly de Jongh and Josephine Wood. *Indian Costumes of Guatemala.* Akademische Druck-u. Verlagsanstalt. Graz/Austria. 1966.

Osgood, Cornelius. *The Ethnography of the Tanaina. Yale University Publications in Anthropology*, no. 16. New Haven: Yale University Press. 1937.

Parker, Chief Everett and Oledoska. *The Secret of No-Face: an Ireokwa Epic.* Healdsburg, California: Native American Publishing Company. 1972.

Pasztory, Esther. *Aztec Stone Sculpture.* New York: The Center for Inter-American Relations. 1976.

Pearlstone, Zena. *Katsina: Commodified and Appropriated Images of Hopi Supernaturals.* Los Angeles: UCLA Fowler Museum of Cultural History. 2001.

Pettit, Robert M. and Florence H. Pettit. *Mexican Folk Toys.* New York: Hastings House. 1978.

Rainey, Froehlich G. *The Whale Hunters of Tigara. Anthropological Papers of the AMNH*, vol. 41, part 2. New York: AMNH. 1947.

Rands, Robert L. and Barbara C. Rands. "Pottery Figurines of the Maya Lowlands." *HMAI* vol. 2, part 1, pp. 535–560. 1965.

_____. "Classic and Postclassic Pottery Figurines of the Guatemalan Highlands." *HMAI*, vol. 2, part 1, pp. 156–162. 1965.

Ray, Dorothy Jean. *Eskimo Art: Tradition and Innovation in Northern*

Alaska. Seattle: University of Washington Press. 1977.

_____. *Aleut and Eskimo Art*. Seattle: University of Washington Press. 1981.

Reichel-Dolmatoff, Gerardo. "Anthropomorphic Figures from Colombia, Their Magic and Art." In *Essays in Pre-Columbian Art and Archaeology*. Ed. Samuel K. Lothrop. Cambridge: Harvard University Press. 1961.

Roosevelt, Anna C. "A Discussion of Chancay Funerary Dolls." *Indian Notes* 8 (1): 18–25. New York: MAI-HF. 1972.

_____. "Interpreting Certain Female Images in Prehistoric Art: The Pretty Ladies." In *Actas del Congreso Internacional de Americanistas*. 1986.

Sandstrom, Alan R. "Paper Spirits of Mexico." *Natural History*, January, pp. 67–72. New York: ANMH. 1986.

Sandstrom, Alan R. and Pamela Effrein Sandstrom. *Traditional Papermaking and Paper Cult Figures of Mexico*. Norman: University of Oklahoma Press. 1986.

Skinner, Alanson B. *Associations and Ceremonies of the Menomini Indians. Anthropological Papers of the AMNH*, vol. 13, part 2. New York: AMNH. 1915.

_____. "Tree-Dweller Bundle of the Wahpeton Dakota." *Indian Notes*, vol. II, pp. 66–73. New York: MAI-HF. 1925.

Snow, Dean. *The Archaeology of North America*. London: Thames and Hudson Ltd. 1980. Originally published 1976.

Stout, David B. *The Cuna*. In *Handbook of South American Indians*, vol. 4, *BAE/B* 143. 1948.

Swan, James G. *The Northwest Coast*. New York: Harper and Brothers. 1857.

Tanner, Clara Lee. *Prehistoric Southwestern Craft Arts*. Tucson: University of Arizona Press. 1976.

Trump, Erik. "'The Idea of Help': White Women Reformers and the Commercialization of Native American Women's Arts." In *Selling the Indian: Commecializing and Appropriating American Indian Cultures*. Eds. Carter Jones Meyer and Diana Royer. Pp. 159–189. Tucson: University of Arizona Press. 2001.

Tuck, James A. "An Archaic Indian Cemetery in Newfoundland." Originally published in *Scientific American*, June, 1970. Reprinted in Zubrow, Fritz, and Fritz.

Voegelin, C. F. *The Shawnee Female Deity. Yale University Publications in Anthropology*. No. 10. New Haven: Yale University Press. 1936.

Weaver, Muriel Porter. *The Aztecs, Maya, and Their Predecessors: Archaeology of Mesoamerica*. New York: Academic Press, a subsidiary of Harcourt Brace Jovanovich. 1981.

West, Patsy. "Glade Cross Mission: An Influence on Florida Seminole Arts and Crafts." *AIA*, vol. 9, no. 4, pp. 58–67. 1984.

White, William L. *A Journey for Margaret*. New York: Harcourt, Brace and Company. 1941.

Wildschut, William. "Crow Sun Dance Bundle." *Indian Notes*, vol. 3, no. 2, pp. 99–107. New York: MAI-HF. 1926.

_____. *Crow Indian Medicine Bundles. Contributions from the MAI/HF* vol. XVII. Ed. John C. Ewers. New York: MAI/HF. 1975.

Willoughby, Charles C. "The Turner Group of Earthworks, Hamilton County, Ohio." *Papers of the Peabody Museum of American Archaeology and Ethnology, Harvard University*, vol. VIII, no. 3. Cambridge: Harvard University. 1922.

van Winning, Hasso. "Figurines with Movable Limbs from Ancient Mexico." *Ethnos* 23(1): 1–60. 1958.

Wissler, Clark. "Ceremonial Bundles of the Blackfoot Indians." *Anthropological Papers of the ANMH*, vol. 7, part 2. New York: AMNH. 1912.

Witthoft, John and Wendell S. Hadlock. "Cherokee-Iroquois Little People." *Journal of American Folklore*, vol. 59, pp. 413–422. 1946.

Wolf, Eric R. *Sons of the Shaking Earth*. Chicago: The University of Chicago Press. 1959.

Wright, Barton. *Hopi Kachinas: The Complete Guide to Collecting Kachina Dolls*. Flagstaff: Northland Press. 1977.

Zubrow, E. B. W., M. C. Fritz, and J. M. Fritz, editors. *New World Archaeology: Theoretical and Cultural Transformations*. San Francisco: W. H. Freeman and Company. 1974.

INDEX